THE
SILENT
QUESTION

BV

Books by Toni Packer

THE
SILENT
QUESTION

Meditating in the
Stillness of Not-Knowing

Toni Packer

Introduction by John V. Canfield

SHAMBHALA
BOSTON & LONDON • 2007

SHAMBHALA PUBLICATIONS, INC.
Horticultural Hall
300 Massachusetts Avenue
Boston, Massachusetts 02115
www.shambhala.com

9 8 7 6 5 4 3 2

Printed in the United States of America

♾ This edition is printed on acid-free paper that
meets the American National Standards
Institute z39.48 Standard.

Distributed in the United States by Random House, Inc.,
and in Canada by Random House of Canada Ltd

Library of Congress Cataloging-in-Publication Data
Packer, Toni 1927–
The silent question: meditating in the stillness of not-knowing / Toni Packer.
p. cm.
ISBN 978-1-59030-410-5 (alk. paper)
1. Meditation. 2. Spiritual life. I. Title.
BL627.P26 2007
204'.4—DC22
2006032789

To Kyle

. . . I beg you . . . to have patience with everything unresolved in your heart and try to love the *questions themselves* as if they were locked rooms or books written in a very foreign language. Don't search right now for the answers, which could not be given you, because you would not be able to live them. And the point is, to live everything. *Live* the questions now. Perhaps then, someday far in the future, you will gradually, without ever noticing it, live your way into the answer.

—RAINER MARIA RILKE

Contents

To the Reader

The Silent Question: Meditating in the Stillness of Not-Knowing contains a collection of talks, dialogues, and interviews that took place over the past several years. It is an attempt to convey to the reader our ways of working together at Springwater Center through presenting observations, questions, and challenges embedded in differing formats. We have repeatedly received requests from our readers to publish group dialogues that take place at the center. This book offers a variety of ways of working together in meditative inquiry.

Let me clarify a few words that are used frequently throughout this book. To my knowledge, the word *awaring* was first used by the Danish mystic Sunyata in his book *Sunyata: The Life and Sayings of a Rare-Born Mystic.*[*] Using the verb form of *awareness* came quite naturally to me from my familiarity with the German word *gewahren*, which means "becoming aware of, noticing, discovering, or seeing." The beauty of the word *gewahren* lies in the fact that it contains the word *wahr*, which means "true."

The word *silence* is not merely intended to denote the absence of words or any kind of noise, but a state of mind that is silently open to perceiving the truth of questioning.

---

[*] Sunyata. *Sunyata: The Life and Sayings of a Rare-Born Mystic*, ed. Betty Cambi and Elliot Isenberg (Berkeley, Calif.: North Atlantic Books, 1990).

The sense in which I use the word *question* in the title of this book is not one of asking for traditional answers but rather denotes a subtle state of mind that does not know but remains open to wondering and freshly perceiving.

Every time I go over the transcript of a talk, it is surprising to discover how different it is to read transcriptions of spoken words *before* they are edited for the printed page. After D Allen completed the first edit of the transcript, I undertook another one, which at times resulted in rewriting (or leaving out) whole paragraphs. It isn't just the difference between speaking and reading words that brings about fresh insights into events and their expressions, but also our own inner unfolding that lets events appear different at different times.

It is not always easy reading words that come out of meditative inquiry. However, when the readers themselves have entered a state of meditative questioning—listening and looking without conclusions already in mind—it will not be difficult to embrace writings that come out of the same mode. Over the years I have found that meditative inquiry that arises out of the depth of *not-knowing* has an amazing way of emptying the mind of ideas, thus revealing its ways of coming upon truth. On the other hand, a question that starts from *knowing* or *guessing* the answer lacks the spontaneity of genuine wondering, probing, and discovering. The beauty of *not-knowing* allows an ever-fresh beginning of a world that need not grow stale under the disguise of knowing.

TONI PACKER

Acknowledgments

HEARTFELT THANKS TO EVERYONE who devoted time and energy to working on *The Silent Question: Meditating in the Stillness of Not-Knowing*.

D Allen offered generous help by selecting, organizing, and pre-editing transcriptions according to an outline he prepared for this new collection of talks, dialogues, and interviews. Besides D Allen's work and the transcribing he did himself, transcriptions were made by Sandy Gray, Susan McCallum, Dennis Peak, and Geoff Swaebe. Kieran Mead-Ward helped with references and citations. Susan McCallum and John Francis gave helpful suggestions. Susan undertook the meticulous job of proofreading and formatting the manuscript. John Francis took care of the many computer problems that happen to someone not skilled in the mysterious ways of this cyber-instrument, and he was of immense help with the whole process of copyediting.

Special thanks to our dear friend of over forty years Jack Canfield, who took time and energy away from his own work to devote to writing an introduction for this book.

I also wish to thank Jennifer Brown of Shambhala Publications, who graciously took over the editing from Emily Bower when Emily's workload demanded cutting back on her schedule.

Lastly, warm gratitude for all the "silent" questions raised by staff, center members, correspondents, retreatants, and visitors to Springwater Center—all the friends, whose genuine curiosity provides a wellspring of inspiration for the pursuit of meditative inquiry.

Introduction

by Jack Canfield[*]

DEATH, DESTRUCTION, UNREASON: being surrounded by these in her childhood awoke in Toni Packer a strong desire to understand the human condition, to find the meaning of life. As she reports in this book:

> "What is the purpose of life?" is not a meaningful question—although this was a question that was driving me tremendously during the war years and prewar years in Hitler Germany. I saw how meaninglessly and senselessly human beings were living, with constant antagonism, conflict, and struggle. They were persecuting and killing each other, and I had to resolve for myself the question of the meaning of life.[†]

At some point in Toni's later sojourn in America the question renewed its grip on her. The search for an answer brought her eventually to the Zen Buddhism practiced at Philip Kapleau's center in Rochester, New York. Later she would change somewhat the

---

[*] John V. Canfield, Professor Emeritus, The University of Toronto at Mississauga, is the author of *Wittgenstein: Language and World* and *The Looking-Glass Self*. He has worked with Toni for over twenty years.

[†] See "Tying Rocks to Clouds" in this book, p. 23.

words in which she preferred to speak of the matter of primary interest to Zen. Instead of *kensho*, or "enlightenment," she would
come to talk of *presence*—awareness of "a simple fact that each one
of us can come upon. See the cloud, the darkness! Hear the wind!
Feel the breathing! Smell the flowers! Touch the swaying grasses!
Clouds, wind, thoughts, breathing, fragrant flowers, and grasses
change all the time, but seeing is here without time."* It is that
timeless "seeing" that resolves the issue of the meaning of life.

The story of Toni's involvement with Zen and later movement
away from it is well known. It is told, for example, in an interview
with her in Lenore Friedman's book *Meetings with Remarkable
Women*. Prior to her coming to the Rochester Zen Center, Toni
had already had several deep experiences of the kind valued in
Zen. At Rochester she made quick progress in koan study, passing
through the koans from the classical collections *Hekigan Roku* and
the *Mumonkan*. Roshi Kapleau acknowledged her understanding
by asking her to take over the center when he retired. She was
clearly marked as the heir apparent. But as things transpired, Toni
eventually had to travel to Mexico, where the Roshi was staying
at the time, to break the news that she could no longer consider
herself a Buddhist. She subsequently left Rochester to establish
what came to be known as the Springwater Center.

Why could she no longer count herself a Buddhist? Well, what
was she rejecting? What was it like to be a Buddhist at Rochester
in those years? In the very earliest period of Philip Kapleau's estab-
lishment and running of the center, I remember him emphasizing
that Zen was a sect of Buddhism and as such it accepted the standard Buddhist doctrines, including those of karma, rebirth, no-self,
and enlightenment. Other features of the Zen practiced at
Rochester concerned action and behavior, from wearing the pre-
scribed brown robes to the esoteric business of praying for succor to

* Toni Packer, *The Wonder of Presence* (Boston: Shambhala Publications,
2002, 2007), p. 157.

Bodhisattvas, in particular Avalokiteshvara, Bodhisattva of Compassion. In addition there were the practices of chanting—in both English and Japanese—bell ringing, incense burning, display of Buddha statues, prostrations to the Buddha and to one's teacher, week-long rigorous retreats modeled on Japanese Zen *sesshins*, the use of the stick or *kyosaku* to keep up the energy in the meditation hall, and meditation involving koans. Toni could no longer be a Buddhist because she could no longer accept a good deal of this amalgam of belief, doctrine, and practice. What she could not support was dropped in her own work at Springwater—although, it should be stressed, some crucial aspects of Rochester Zen were retained.

As for doctrine, Toni continued to acknowledge two of the four tenets of Buddhism I mentioned: no-self and enlightenment. But the point is easily misunderstood. Her acceptance is not intellectual, but is rather based on, and is to be understood in terms of, a person's own experience. No-self and enlightenment can be realized in one's life. That emphasis on *direct realization, oneness*, or an immediate *presence*, and her corresponding avoidance of dogma of all stripes, are hallmarks of her approach. And as in Zen, the emphasis is not on words but on what actually lies before one's eyes.

In appealing to a direct awareness of mind, Toni's work is compatible with a scientific-minded empiricism. Being raised in a secular household, and coming to see science as a central (though not the only) arbiter of truth, may have made it easier for her to leave to one side the nonempirical accoutrements of Zen, such as the doctrine of rebirth. But her approach is also consistent with traditional religious doctrines in the Western tradition, such as the assertion of the existence of God. It is consistent with these various doctrines because they simply are not its concern. What is of concern, one might say, is a direct realization of a *this* that lies outside all conceptualization. In Toni's work, as in that of many other spiritual leaders, such a realization can effect a deep transformation in one's life, a movement from the duality of self-and-other to a oneness. That oneness is articulated, for example, in Krishna-murti's remark that "the observer is the observed," or in Huang Po's reference to "a perception, sudden as blinking, that subject and object are one."*

One of the things Toni retained from her Zen days, although in a modified form, was that central element of Zen practice, the lengthy silent retreat, or *sesshin*. At Rochester it included compulsory periods of meditation along with some features mentioned earlier, including the use of the *kyosaku*. Springwater retreats with Toni, on the other hand, eventually dropped all of these features except for daily talks by her, individual meetings, and the all-important silence. The result is a simplified form of retreat that proceeds in an unconstrained and natural manner and provides an opportunity for direct contemplative inquiry into mind.

The themes of no-self, enlightenment, and the meaning of life are all connected. To be enlightened is, in Toni's words, *presence*. Presence resolves the issue of the meaning of life. The illusion of self ceases.

Concerning the self as illusion, Toni writes, for example:

> Now, is there such an entity as *me* or *I*? Or is it just like the weather—an ongoing, ever changing stream of ideas, images, memories, projections, likes and dislikes . . . that thought keeps calling *I, me, Toni,* and thereby solidifying what is evanescent?†

Toni's view is that thought, here, has created an illusion. But, to elaborate a point made earlier, it is important to understand the nature of that denial of the "I." There are two ways of taking Toni's remark, one intellectual and the other, as we might say, ex-

---

* *The Zen Teaching of Huang Po*, trans. John Blofeld (New York: Grove Press, 1958), p. 92.
† *The Wonder of Presence*, pp. 43–44.

istential. The intellectual mode would place Toni's comments within the long philosophical and social-scientific tradition in which people define "self" in some way or other, and then give reasons for or against its reality. It has been said, for example by Lichtenberg and again by Nietzsche and Wittgenstein, that the self is a non-thing the grammar of our language fools us into positing. Toni's remarks are not meant as contributions to that intellectual issue of the self as illusion. Rather they concern a direct realization. The existential, as opposed to the intellectual, problem is to resolve the question of the meaning of life by directly realizing the reality obscured by our "I"-thoughts.

As regards that centering on the "I," one of the first things meditation, or quiet sitting, makes clear is that our lives are spent in a more or less constant inner involvement with the story of ourselves. The mind, we come to see, is always in motion, turning about the central point of self. The mind's "I"-fostered turbulence was nicely described by La Rochefoucauld:

> The sea may be fairly compared to it, in the tireless ebb and flow of whose waves self-love finds an accurate image of its own seething thoughts and its eternal restlessness.

The "I"-directed thoughts reflect the fundamental division we make between ourselves and the rest of the world: between me and not-me. The concern for self is correspondingly ever-present, or virtually so. That concern brings trouble in its wake. Fear of death, for example, or the inward or outward bad results of anger or hatred. The liberating denial of that seemingly ever-present self is not an intellectual matter. Hatred of those who thwart us, for example, is not put to rest by the thought that the "I" is an illusion. But, Toni writes, there is a solution:

> . . . There is an entirely different way of being when everything appears *completely all right the way it is!* At the instant

of total presence (absence of separation), there is no need for the brain to produce phantasmagorias—interpretations of what this could mean to "me," "my" friends, or "my" foes. It is possible to change from interpreting everything according to old patterns of the past. . . .

There is another possibility of relaxing into not-knowing and not interpreting whatever scenarios have been produced by the conceptualizing brain. It's a giant step! Not from here to there, but right here, on the spot! A giant "step" from the suffering me—suffering from all the actual pains and imagined problems—to *just being here* without knowing, predicting, or reflecting about the past, what it was like or what it meant, or what it means right now. . . .*

These remarks may seem strange. What is this giant step that is not from here to there but here to . . . here? A giant step that does not take one out of the place one is already at? In asking those questions we are taking the wrong approach. The "just being here" Toni speaks of is something that resists or balks the knowing mind. Here reason seems to have reached an end. Understandably enough, for the alternative to I-centered concern Toni speaks of is nothing intellectual. The alternative amounts to what I called an existential solution to the problem of the meaning of life. It is a matter of presence, or—not to mince words—enlightenment. Toni writes:

Enlightenment, True Nature, True Self, Wholeness, the Unconditioned Absolute—whatever words have been given to what is without words, unthinkable, unknowable, ungraspable—is not the effect of a cause. It is luminously present and timeless, overlooked by the roving intellect

---

* See "Has Toni Packer Been Totally Transformed?" in this book, pp. 172–173.

that is trying to grasp it, and obscured by the bodymind's constantly shifting moods, desires, and fears. Moment-to-moment meditation is clearly coming upon this roving and shifting, resisting and fearing mind and the urge to do something about it! . . . Meditation that is free and effortless, without goal, without expectation, is an expression of Pure Being that has nowhere to go, nothing to get.*

The message of reason must be that in the matter of the meaning of life, reason has no message. The solution—enlightenment, or presence—is not something you can wrap up nicely in a proposition and pass on to others; it's beyond words. So could one say it is a change in one's mode of being? But didn't the Buddha say that out of supreme enlightenment he brought us *nothing*? A changed mode of being is not nothing. So what can we say? Perhaps that the leaves and berries are shiny in the rain? But Toni can say, or not-say, it much better than I.

---

* See "Is Enlightenment a Myth?" in this book, pp. 164–165.

part one

THIS FREE
AND OPEN "WORK"

I

Staying Present

An Interview with Toni Packer
by Geoff Swaebe[*]

There is no need for awareness to turn anywhere. It's here! Everything is here in awareness! When there is a waking up from fantasy, there is no one who does it. Awareness and the sound of a plane are here with no one in the middle trying to "do" them or bring them together. They are here together! The only thing that keeps things (and people) apart is the "me"-circuit with its separative thinking. When that is quiet, divisions do not exist.

GEOFF SWAEBE: You once spoke of a moment many years ago when you were driving to the Rochester Zen Center to have *dokusan* [a formal meeting with a Zen teacher] with Roshi Kapleau. You described a moment when you were looking at the clouds, and I've been trying to understand that moment better.

TONI PACKER: It is a very vivid memory—driving in the evening with shadows long and intense. The sky was blue, and an even wall of clouds stretched along the horizon carved by deep

---

* Geoff Swaebe is an author and retired attorney. He lives in Chestnut Ridge, New York.

shadows that gave the impression of snow-covered mountains. For a moment the brain wanted to move into pleasant memories of Switzerland—vacationing and hiking in the glacier-covered mountains. But instead of getting lost in that, it remained with the driving—the steering wheel in hands, feet on pedals, landscape passing by, clouds along the distant horizon. The awareness was palpable. And yet there was no intention to be or to remain aware—no desire to do "the right thing." It just happened spontaneously: awareness of a strong impulse to shift into a pleasurable memory that is different from simple being here. Being here is just what is.

GEOFF: Is this different from the experience of finding ourselves in a daydream while driving and then returning our attention back to the highway?

TONI: It wasn't the experience of "finding myself in a daydream." It was clear awareness of almost sliding into the daydream yet staying present. There was a clear distinction between being present and entering into the tunnel of remembrance. I hadn't previously noticed this crucial instant of almost shifting into a fantasy and, by seeing clearly, not going with the temptation, without any moral judgment or injunction. Seeing and staying here was not a process—it was instantaneous, without any time involved.

I think that this may actually reveal the answer to whether we need to continue living the way we do. In other words, it is possible to see and feel the arising of a compelling image—almost getting caught up in it and yet not needing to go with it due to the clarity of seeing. Seeing the whole thing in a flash is the change we are all searching for so passionately! The beauty of that!

To give another example: in clearly seeing that I am about to get compulsively entangled in self-defense—for instance, protecting my self-image from getting hurt by someone's disparaging talk, in clearly awaring defensiveness and the self-image that is being defended—can it all abate right then and there at the instant of seeing? Getting caught up in an emotional reaction may be averted by clearly seeing reactivity without any intention to do right or wrong. Just staying here, aware, is enough.

GEOFF: You once used the phrase "the intelligence of it all" to describe this discernment between staying here and being captured by imagery. Why do you characterize it as intelligence?

TONI: I am sure that I had read or heard Krishnamurti's statement that intelligence is operating in presence and awareness. This experience of driving to Rochester one evening was a clear demonstration of it. There was no discernible intention to stay attentive to my driving or to abstain from daydreaming, no "me" directing what to do. It was the instantaneous functioning of something that can appropriately be called "intelligence"—the intelligence of staying here and not getting distracted, yet without anyone giving instructions. This whole thing took care of itself in an intelligent way, working itself out without any doer.

Doesn't Being Present Require Some Doing?

GEOFF: You often refer to the "absence of effort" that characterizes presence or awareness. But it still seems to me that there is some sort of "turning" or "returning" of attention that is involved.

TONI: Well, let's try to clarify it right here and now, together. [An airplane is flying overhead.] The sound of a plane! Both the thought/word plane and, maybe, a mental image of it are right here—aren't they? There is no one doing any attending. Just the sound, the image! [silence] But you were asking, "Isn't the attention turning toward something?" Is it? Let's look and listen! [silence] Can't discern any turning, can you? There is no need for awareness to turn anywhere. It's here! Everything is here in awareness! When there is a waking up from fantasy, there is no one who does it. Awareness and the sound of a plane are here with no one in the middle trying to "do" them or bring them together. They are here together! The only thing that keeps things (and people) apart is the "me"-circuit with its separative thinking. When that is quiet, divisions do not exist.

GEOFF: But aren't there also examples where someone turns attention to a thought, for example of something that happened in the past? Isn't there "a doing" or an effort of some sort that involves the turning of the attention?

TONI: When you can't remember the name of someone, there seems to be an effort in trying to remember it. Thought says, "What was that name! What was it? Was it this or was it that? I've got to remember it!" And there may be some sort of mental straining. But usually nothing much happens on demand. Sooner or later, when thinking/talking about something else, the name crops up because the brain has continued to search quietly, not resting until that which was lost has been found.

You ask, "Isn't there someone turning a thought toward something that has happened in the past?" As long as we are not aware of the ten thousand thoughts circulating throughout the brain, we talk about it as though there was an "I" searching for a memory of the past. Language introduces "duality"—me and mine. But is there really an entity—a "me"—doing this, or is it rather a complex thinking process taking place in the brain and its connected places throughout the body?

Meditative awareness reveals the thought process running its course. It becomes more and more transparent the more the meditative mind unfolds and prevails. Krishnamurti used to say, "The brain wants order." Careful observation reveals this to be exactly so. When a forgotten item is not found, the urge to find it keeps on going subconsciously. As long as a problem is not resolved, it may hang in the mind as "unfinished business," with an amazing driving power. This mind (I can vouch for it!) does not like unfinished business; it wants order, quietly doing its thing of maintaining life. Presence is order—no searching for anything else is needed.

Is Seeing Thoughts and Reactions Enough to Stay Present?

GEOFF: Sometimes you also use the phrase "seeing in awareness" to describe this process. Are you referring to the interplay between body and mind where you can actually see your body's reactions to thought?

TONI: Absolutely! Yes. To behold one initial thought mobilizing this whole body with anger or resentment, anxiety or sadness!

GEOFF: And is the seeing of this body-mind interaction enough to put an end to such thoughts and reactions?

TONI: No. What is needed is coming upon an intelligence that not only sees the constant interplay of thoughts, emotions, stress, and conflict but deeply understands the falseness and deception of self-image with its defensiveness. I don't know how to characterize it other than to say intelligence, intelligent presence that understands cause and effect clearly.

GEOFF: Is there a moment in the seeing of this interplay between the body and thought when thought and the ego abate?

TONI: Yes. It happens when, instead of fighting thoughts with thoughts, they are seen, understood, and left alone. They are like a swarm of mosquitoes, coming and going in their season. But there is something else that we call the gathering of energy in listening, attending, and discovering. It is nothing that the striving ego can bring about. I don't know what brings it about. Nothing brings it about. It happens on its own. And yet, coming to retreats, sitting quietly, attending, and learning about ourselves and others is part and parcel of this whole discovery. So where is the abating of thoughts and connected emotions? You've probably noticed that the more you want to attain such a state, the farther away it gets —the less accessible it becomes. It's when the mind gives up struggling that simple presence reveals itself—not the expected fireworks of enlightenment but the sound of air-conditioning, the buzzing insects, the breathing—all of it happening in silent space. Has it happened to you in retreat—coming upon that amazing stillness?

GEOFF: It has.

TONI: It is amazing, isn't it? Every time it happens, all I can say is, "What marvelous stillness." And some people tell me later, "Yes, I could feel it; it was right there." Here it is. It's here. Everything takes place in stillness even though it seems so far away when there is no abating of the discursive mind. So, just to watch silently and not get lost in the evaluation of one's own condition, which is just more mosquitoes! Have you ever experimented with not reacting, not swatting, not complaining about mosquitoes but just letting them do their thing? Watch a mosquito land on your arm and drink until its tiny belly is overextended with blood. It takes off like a drunken aviator! Roshi Kapleau used to tell us that this was one of the evening practices in a Japanese temple—the head monk opening all the screens and inviting the hungry guests to come in.

Don't We Have to Overcome Resistance to Stay Present?

GEOFF: Is it really possible to see our own resistance at work?

TONI: Yes. If the desire is alive to be intimate with all that is going on internally, resistance can become quite transparent, although not in the form that we expect. It may just be a commonplace reaction like "I don't want to do that," or it may be the body bracing in a nonverbal "no!" It's so commonplace that we don't often become aware of it. When you see a thought and the instant bodily reaction to it becomes transparent, do you also realize that nobody is involved in willing that?

GEOFF: That it's just happening?

TONI: That it's just happening right here. That's clear, isn't it?

GEOFF: Yes.

TONI: And I feel it is also important that we acknowledge freely to ourselves that it's just happening automatically, without any "me" having intended it. In that way the seemingly solid assumption that I'm doing the thinking and I'm reacting can turn into wondering, "If no doer is found, why do I nevertheless feel so strongly that there is one? Why is it so hard to realize that a reaction just happened automatically?" That "I am in control" is just an idea, an assumption. That assumption erodes by realizing that the reaction took place even though this "I" didn't want it to happen like that. But here it is nevertheless. So where is that "I" that feels so omnipotent in thinking, "I can control things," when it can't even control the thoughts and emotional reactions that arise?

GEOFF: When we find ourselves in conflict with something in our environment—someone in our family, a business colleague, a friend—is our desire for change in that environment, or our desire for someone else to change, always a signal that it is the "me"-feeling that is acting out?

TONI: I think it is. Because ego, in its most general terms, is resistance to what is. And in the resistance we think that we are independent doers and that others are too—"If they only wanted to, they could do better," or "If they only tried harder, they could do better," or "If I tried, I could become better." These are examples of thoughts that separate. But if there is a wholesome presence, there is also the realization that things are the way they are due to everything that is going on and has been going on since time immemorial. And everything that has been going on is manifesting as this in this moment. This moment is the result of all that has been going on. If that realization is clear, then there isn't the urge to change others. Maybe just the urge to understand with compassion.

True change comes out of this openness. It is this intelligent realization that we talked about earlier. And maybe there is an action that comes out of this presence that is appropriate to conditions, not springing from heady stuff about the way things ought to be but unfolding out of an apprehension of the whole thing and an appropriate wholesome response. Then it will have the quality of love and compassion. Not born out of the irritation, or the resentment, about the way someone else happens to be behaving.

Now, I know that this is putting it in seemingly idealistic terms, because usually we are not completely whole, completely here. But if there is conflict, there can also be an immediate wondering, "Is there a resistance here to what is? And why? Is it necessary? Is it possible to just flow with what is?" If the desire is there to really be intimate with resistance, it will happen, although perhaps not in the form that we expect. It is such a relief not to have to change other people or the world but to flow and let a compassionate response come out of this flow.

2

Fear of Silence

You ask, "Is this silence the absence of noise or is it qualitatively different?" Whom are you asking? Everyone here? How about asking it of yourself? To yourself.

[*The group sits in silence for several minutes.*]

TONI PACKER: Here you don't have to raise your hands to speak.

PARTICIPANT 1: This is my first retreat, and I'm having some difficulty with the . . . uh . . . issue of silence. I'm someone who can live very well without the radio, TV, the Internet . . . and, uh, while I've been happily married for many years, I can be by myself and I'm used to doing things by myself. I came here knowing this was a silent retreat, and I had certain expectations about how I might respond in a silent environment. But it has been different than I expected . . . and the issue I want to bring up for this group is the nature of the silence that we've experienced—or at least that I've experienced—on first impression here at Springwater. I find it a different phenomenon, a totally different phenomenon, than the type of quiet—absence of noise—that one can sometimes experience outside of retreat. I think this silence here is a double-edged sword. On the one side, I find it somewhat menacing. I was just thinking that the deep silence here is like being swallowed—in Shakespeare's terms—by the giant maw of death. You know, where the character's last words are, "The rest is silence." So I'm responding to the notion of silence here as something that is really different, and I find it spiritually therapeutic, but I also find it spiritually claustrophobic. I'm struggling. . . . I . . . I find myself more vulnerable than I thought I would be. I'm trying to work out a way to deal with it. Uh . . . to put it intellectually, on that level . . . is the silence experienced here compared to the silence experienced outside of retreat a difference of degree or of kind? A second question I have is how many of you found this silence threatening or menacing or disconcerting, as I have?

PARTICIPANT 2: Can you specify what you mean by "disconcerting"? I mean, is it scary or is it just kind of nebulous or—?

PARTICIPANT 1: *Anxiety* is a good word. I think there's a difference between fear of the dark . . . something we easily understand psychologically . . . it's dark and there's something dangerous and something's going to come out and attack you. That's the standard fairy tale of the dark. I think this is different. I think this is like . . . well, that quote from Shakespeare or . . . the Great Void, or the notion of something that you'll drown in. It's not something that's going to attack you. It's not that kind of fear. It's like . . . writers talk about fear of the ocean in which we can drown. So it's like anxiety about drowning.

TONI: What is it that could drown?

PARTICIPANT 1: Ah! Well, I don't want to be clever . . . the self?

TONI: In linking back to your very first question—"Is this silence the absence of noise or is it qualitatively different?"—whom are you asking? Everyone here? How about asking it of yourself? To yourself.

PARTICIPANT 1: I did.

TONI: Oh. But it's only the second day of retreat—

PARTICIPANT 1: I don't mean to be presumptuous, Toni—

TONI: No, I didn't mean . . . I didn't think you were presumptuous. [*pause*] Everyone here could give you descriptions—and I don't want to be in the way of people giving you descriptions and explanations of this silence, which is qualitatively different from absence of noise—but what good is it to you if we tell you? You don't know whether we speak from direct experience or from what is indirect, heard. So can it be an alive question for you? What is the nature of this silence that seems to be as threatening as the idea of death, of drowning? Are you interested in asking that question of yourself?

PARTICIPANT 1: I'm interested both on an intellectual level, which is the way I posed it first—

TONI: I understand.

PARTICIPANT 1: —but also there's an emotional level. I'm interested in both.

TONI: Does anyone wish to respond?

PARTICIPANT 3: Well . . . menacing or not . . . is there a willingness to experience the silence, however it comes?

PARTICIPANT 1: I think . . . the answer . . . well, the silence is here; one doesn't have much choice.

TONI: Well, the brain can turn on a lot in this silence, one video after another—memories, expectations, judgments, commentary. It can just animate the silence with all kinds of stuff. The brain is incredibly creative at that. That's what you're experiencing in the silence, aren't you?

PARTICIPANT 1: I don't know if my brain has been playing internal videotapes. I think it's responding immediately to the environment . . . emotions are evoked . . . I think they're very primary emotions, because—

TONI: But the question was, "Is there any choice but to face this silence, to explore it and what comes up in it?" And you said, "There is no choice—"

PARTICIPANT 1: [loud] I said silence is "choiceless."

TONI: Well, is there silence, or is there the idea of silence? Is the silence you speak about the absence of noise or . . . ?

PARTICIPANT 1: My only response, after today, is that the difference is in kind rather than in degree. I see it as a different

phenomenon than quiet moments—moments without noise—
outside of retreat. And that's why it's puzzling.

TONI: . . . and "threatening," you say.

PARTICIPANT 1: Yes, I said that.

TONI: Yes, "the ocean," "death." But these are still ideas, aren't
they? So is that what we're afraid of . . . the ideas that crop up
about the silence? We're very good at scaring ourselves through a
description or story. You talked about that very well.

PARTICIPANT 4: When I come here, it's such a relief, the silence. Last week, at home . . . we have some neighbors who moved
in recently and it's a very quiet neighborhood, across from a big
park, and I really treasure the quietness of it. These new neighbors
are very much into their music, and just this last weekend they had
this music blaring until two A.M., and I just could not fall asleep.
It was OK music, but it was really annoying to me . . . and I wonder
if my experience of the music and the noise is similar to your reaction to silence. I wonder if it's the same kind of thing . . . though for
me it almost feels like a grating on the nerves, that kind of thing. It
also sets up the feeling of a violation of my personal space, something forced on me that I haven't chosen to participate in. So it
brings up a lot of reactions—and questions—about me as a separate entity, and about having stuff come at me that I don't choose
to be there. I don't know if this is different from how the silence
feels to you. I know that, for me, when I come here to retreat, I
don't have to deal with all that, and it feels like such a relief to me.
[pauses] Although . . . last night I thought I heard some music—
probably from a car radio—and I immediately thought, "What is
that? Who's invading my space? That shouldn't be here. This is the
silence place."

PARTICIPANT 1: Well, since I couldn't talk to anyone last night
about this, I looked at Larry Rosenberg's newest book, and he has
in it a section on silence, being in silence. Some of what I've been
experiencing he deals with in this book. Is there any objection if
I read a little of it? Toni?

Toni: You don't need to be given permission here.

Participant 1: He put his finger on a couple of things . . . and of course he dealt with it at the level of someone who's been a practitioner for many years. Can I read a passage or two?

Participant 5: Yes.

Participant 1: [*He reads a section from the Larry Rosenberg's* Breath by Breath *(Boston: Shambhala Publications, 1998), ending with*] " . . . I had a number of students who had progressed quite far in their meditation practice and had reached the threshold of deep silence, but had encountered a profound fear and pulled back. With the goal of seeing students progress as far as they could, I asked myself how to deal with what was holding them back." So here is someone talking about this silence and the fear it can bring up. I don't know if this helps focus it a little better. . . .

Participant 6: I live a fairly quiet life, too. But there is something different about living with a group of people in silence, even for a week. I heard somebody before the retreat explaining why they recommended not reading and writing during the retreat, and I thought, "Well, that's interesting; let me see if I can do that." I didn't know if I could go a whole week without reading, so I decided I'd try it for one day. What I found is that it made the silence even more profound. I then had to deal with "What am I going to do, how can I just be?" I feel like not reading and writing is helping me go a little deeper . . . allowing stuff to come up into view . . . and I don't necessarily feel scared about it. . . .

Participant 1: I think he [Rosenberg] would agree with that. At his retreats there is no reading of any kind, and no writing in journals or anything, just for the reason you've said. I think it's so you can experience it yourself . . . thank you.

Toni: So, [Participant 1], let's take your experience of this fear of silence. I take it you aren't just inventing this. You're describing something that has happened to you sometime in these last two days.

Participant 1: Last night.

Toni: Last night. Now, how to meet that anxiety, that fear? Going down to the library, which we have here with all the many donated books—does that help allay the fear? Now you have the written word. You read somebody and feel some manner of support and security. Another possibility is that there may be a moment where there is no choice but to meet this fear that has threaded its way through our whole life . . . and fear is not the only thing repressed. Here in a retreat it can surface. We talked about it yesterday. Is it part of the functioning of retreat to bring up into view what has been repressed, kept at bay, forgotten? And to meet that by being in its presence? The mind wants to know, "What can I do about it? I have to do something to get rid of it." Instead . . . just be in the presence of what's there and let it speak to you. You can ask it questions: "Why am I so afraid?" Maybe it's the thought of death, or being swallowed by the ocean, drowning. And if you ask a question like this, then be quiet. Ask the question into darkness, into a bottomless well. "Why am I so afraid? What makes me so upset?" . . . and then quietly listen. Something may bubble up . . . "I'm afraid of this or that" . . . and then quiet and listening again. Not immediately explaining it away. "Is that what I'm afraid of?" Then quiet again. And maybe see what else is there . . . because this fear of death or drowning, or whatever, is not the whole thing. Ask with interest, with openness, determined not to hold back. Let the whole thing show itself. Even at the risk of being swallowed. Usually we're just swallowed by our thoughts and memories, not by presence. Presence doesn't swallow us. It just is; it's here. [pause] Which doesn't mean to not go down to the library and read. At the right time, a pregnant phrase can strike us and open us, not just to the words but to what the words point to.

Participant 1: I appreciate your comments. They're helpful. I like reading because it explains things on a rational level. I like to approach things first and foremost rationally. But I understand that's not the whole answer in dealing with these things, and perhaps your suggestion is a good next step. Thanks.

TONI: The rational level definitely has its place and its function. Sometimes to have something explained or described very
rationally so that it makes sense to the intellect . . . for one thing,
that dissipates false ideas . . . and maybe lets the intellect relax.
Then, maybe, for once you can see something directly, not through
thoughts and ideas, false assumptions. Still, the rational mind has
to expose its own limitations. But it's probably of limited value to
say this. You have to see it for yourself, what its functioning is and
what its limitations are. That's the beauty of this work, to ulti-
mately find out for oneself.

PARTICIPANT 3: [after a pause] Your mind may be in a panic
while you're at the same time very carefully and quietly coming
and going in and out of this room. So something is functioning
that isn't in the least bit afraid. . . .

PARTICIPANT 1: Thanks for saying that. I raised my concern
about the silence here at retreat . . . well, don't take it as a criti-
cism . . . my overall response to the retreat has been very positive.
That's why I feel comfortable raising this specific thing, because it
has been a very nice experience so far. Thanks.

[long pause]

TONI: Maybe, sometimes, more frightening than the silence is
everything it allows to come up and be questioned . . . all the stuff
about the way we live. It's not a matter of finding fault, but simply
looking, seeing . . . this is what I'm doing, this is how I'm living.
Something comes up . . . greed, anger, guilt. To behold it as part of
this conditioning is one thing, but to think, "Oh my God, I'm not
like that; I don't want to be like that. . . ." or to rationalize it away,
or create explanations for why I'm this way. . . . That's where the
fear comes in: one reacts with disturbance that one could be like
that! But to simply look at all these reactions and emotions coming up, see that this is what it is to be a human being . . . see that
it's like this for all of us, including myself. So, can we dis-identify
from what is seen, moment to moment . . . ?

3

Effortlessness

Unless effortlessness prevails, you cannot help making an effort!

PARTICIPANT 1: Earlier in the meeting [Participant 2] brought up the question of effort—the difficulty of sitting with pain and discomfort and the sense that this takes a lot of effort. [Participant 2], you felt that in agreeing with that, Toni had contradicted what she usually says—that this work is without effort. We didn't have a chance to go into that at the time.

PARTICIPANT 2: Yeah. I remember.

PARTICIPANT 1: But it brought the question up for me again. When I think of "no effort," I think of awareness, simply being here, the listening, sounds, breathing, just . . . the silence of it all. But . . . [long pause] . . . the other thing I realized in looking at it— and I'm being really honest here—is that I didn't come to that silence without a lot of effort.

TONI PACKER: To be sure.

PARTICIPANT 1: I mean, back at a Zen center, the first sesshin I went to, maybe thirty years ago—and I don't mind sharing this, it's no big deal really—well, at first I didn't even go to dokusan. And then finally it was coming near the end of the first day and I hadn't gone yet. So the teacher's assistants actually got me into the dokusan room, and the first thing the teacher asked was,

"Why haven't you come here before now? Don't you want enlightenment?" And I remember thinking, "Well, what's wrong with where I'm at?" You know? [*laughs*] But it was part of the teacher's job to light that fire, to light the whole sesshin on fire, and so I got into it. Got so much into it that by the last night—sitting there with a friend, and the whole competitive thing going on of course—I stayed up the entire night and didn't even go to the morning meal. I'd been to a lot of dokusans by then, done a lot of so-called demonstrations [of Zen understanding], including knocking the teacher over—everything I'd probably read about what you do when you come before your teacher. But that next morning . . . I can still remember it, though it's thirty years ago. *Completely* consumed with this question [who am I?] . . . I was walking, not sitting but walking in the meditation line, and everything went black. This brain . . . all I can say is, this brain had completely shut down. Then there was a birdsong . . . and . . . it was like an explosion . . . and the tears and . . . just . . . being here. Tremendous effort and energy had gone on in this bodymind [*laughs*]—but now I still think of hearing the birdsong and in that all the effort had been consumed, and then there was just the relief. Which is probably why there was crying, because of the relief of being here.

TONI: Being here without effort!

PARTICIPANT 1: Yes. Uh . . . so, after all this talking [*laughs*] . . .

TONI: Remember my saying, "Unless effortlessness prevails, you cannot help making an effort!"

PARTICIPANT 1: Uh-huh.

TONI: It's the way our constitution and conditioning work. So when people speak about effortlessness, either it's a concept or they *are* truly in that state of no effort. Just openness without "me."

I should not speak against making an effort because I, too, made a prodigious effort during Zen training. And yet I cannot say that *because* I made that effort in the past I am where I am today! There are many unfathomable things going on: working

strenuously toward a goal and suddenly realizing that we are completely here—have been here all the time!

PARTICIPANT 1: We can't say it's impossible without effort.

TONI: No! The example yesterday of the marine who was making no effort "to get enlightened"—he hadn't ever heard about
that kind of thing! He told me that it took all the strength he
could muster to climb up the stairs into the helicopter that would
take him on a mission he thought was certain death. It was the
effort of having to fight the powerful urge for self-preservation—
fighting the paralyzing fear of death.

Total presence is entirely different—it is without fight or resistance, without fear, without the "me." Is it the result of a cause?

The way you describe the efforts of your first sesshin sounds
like an overwhelming drive against resistance resulting in an explosion—nothing left to beat against.

PARTICIPANT 1: Yes.

TONI: Often people in sesshin feel as if they are hitting hard
against an immovable wall, but *oneself* is that wall, you know, and
when that has crumbled, there's nothing left but openness.

But—it doesn't necessarily *have to be* that kind of a path.

PARTICIPANT 1: No, no. Making that kind of effort may not be
relevant to where one is at. That's what I see or hear sometimes
from people . . . it's the wanting to do something that doesn't
really resonate well with where one is at. One is pretty much here
already! [*laughs*] I mean, I was gone; I remember being so completely shut down before that happened. So . . . at least that's the
way I see it. It just seems that if somebody isn't in such a shut-
down place, then . . .

TONI: Does that raise the question again, for disciple as well as
teacher: "Do we need to follow a path because it has worked for
others before?"

[*Toni turns to another participant.*] Like the traditional practices
you talked about earlier. Aren't they also predicated on totally ex-
hausting the mind?

PARTICIPANT 3: Yeah. I remember something like you described when, after a teaching, there was a lama just sitting there for several minutes. It seemed as though the sky opened. There was no effort there. [*laughs*]

TONI: Yes, the teaching had been going on, and then there was just sitting completely still . . .

PARTICIPANT 3: Yeah.

TONI: . . . and so was your mind. [*chuckles*] Quieted down, wasn't it?

PARTICIPANT 3: Yes.

TONI: Yes, I understand that.

PARTICIPANT 3: You don't know what caused it.

TONI: Because *this* is always here! The Buddhists call it our True Mind. How can it have a cause, a past, a future? It's always here, beyond all time.

PARTICIPANT 1: All that being said, if someone said they *wanted* to make an effort, it's unlikely I would tell them not to explore that. That's one of the things about being here at Springwater retreat—the possibility to try things out and, in the process, to find out for oneself.

TONI: Yes, yes. Likewise, a lot of people come here who have spent a lot of time with exhaustive "efforting" and now appreciate simply being here quietly, watching the ways of exertion or no exertion without "knowing." Just beholding it all—seeing through it all!

The rest is silence.

4

Tying Rocks to Clouds

An Interview with Toni Packer
by William Elliott*

What I am concerned with is what is going on right now in the human being. Can there be an open, free awareness of this? That is not the case if one postpones being in touch with it now for the sake of getting enlightenment in the future.

WILLIAM ELLIOTT: On what beliefs do you base your life?

TONI PACKER: I don't base my life on any belief.

WILLIAM: If you had a friend who felt the need for some beliefs to base life on, what would you tell the friend?

TONI: I would wonder if my friend was interested in finding out why this need to have a belief exists, whether there is fear or insecurity. Why not be in touch with this fear and insecurity and see if one can get to the root of that, rather than escape into these beliefs? There is no belief system in my life.

---

* William Elliott is the author of *Tying Rocks to Clouds*. He devotes most of his time to traveling in his motor home, interviewing spiritual leaders, and giving talks at universities, hospices, churches, and bookstores. He makes his home in Madison, WI.

Look out there. [*She points out the window.*] The sun is about to set. Do you have to believe that? The wind is blowing; the snow is swirling. Do you have to believe that? If you see something is so, it is so. If you don't see it, you are afraid, and then you have to believe. I feel having ideals is a very dangerous thing for human beings. We have ideals because we have lost the ability to see directly. Ideals may create conflict. Your ideals might be different from my ideals, and therefore we are at odds with each other. Let's find out what the truth is and not indulge in speculating about our ideals. Watch the mind. Do we have an awareness of the processes? What is an ideal? It is thought. It is conditioning and is taken from others. But what is the truth? That is what interests me, not ideals. Can there be listening without ideals, without beliefs, without the separation of me and what I'm listening to? Just simple, open listening? It can't be put into words. Words are very limiting.

WILLIAM: Do you think there is a purpose to life?

TONI: "What is the purpose of life?" is not a meaningful question—although this was a question that was driving me tremendously during the war years and prewar years in Hitler Germany. I saw how meaninglessly and senselessly human beings were living, with constant antagonism, conflict, and struggle. They were persecuting and killing each other, and I had to resolve for myself the question of the meaning of life.

But the one who asks this question feels separate from life: "me" and "my life." Because of this separation there is this haunting question, "What is the meaning of life?" When there is no feeling of separation, then there is just living. There is just life. No one is standing outside of life and therefore worrying about whether this is pointed toward something else. Everything is what it is; it doesn't point toward something else.

WILLIAM: You seem to be refuting the questions I am asking. It makes me feel as though the questions are ridiculous.

TONI: That is quite all right. As you said in the beginning, these questions are the questions we ask.

WILLIAM: What would you say is the greatest obstacle to truth?

TONI: Truth has no obstacles. You mean the *perception* of truth and understanding. The greatest obstacle is this deeply ingrained sense of self, of "me"—the deeply ingrained sense that I am a separate individual, separate from everyone else, and all that goes with that sense of separation. We believe we are separate because we are deceived by our thoughts, images, ideas, ideals, and sensations. Do you believe it? We must believe it because it feels that way, doesn't it? Are you interested in finding out what makes for this strong feeling and belief that there is a separate self? If that question grabs you, then you will begin to observe what makes for that feeling of separation, the thoughts that come up, the feelings and emotions in that relationship.

We have an image of "what I am, what I was, what I could be, and what I should be." What people think of me and what I want them to see in me has a tremendously strong hold on the mind and the body. All ideas and images are made up and come out of memory, which is connected with deep emotions and sensations. This in turn affects our perception of people and things.

Suffering is connected with this sense of self. There is suffering because we are sufferers or because we feel victimized. It has to do with the sense of "me" and what is happening to "me." If that sense of self isn't there, then pain is pain and sorrow is sorrow, and we are not the sufferer of that. But this doesn't mean no depth of feeling. We can feel feeling for the sorrow of humankind, but it is not pity or self-pity but seeing what we do to ourselves and each other.

WILLIAM: Do you have any ideas about enlightenment?

TONI: Enlightenment is not an idea. If an idea about enlightenment is carried around, it affects our action. We want it and will do anything to get it; we will submit to any kind of discipline or system to get that enlightenment. But in the process of trying to get the enlightenment, we will not be in touch with what is actually going on. For instance, there is wanting, lacking, having a goal, striving, and competition—all because of wanting enlightenment. So what I am concerned with is what is going on right now in the human being. Can there be an open, free awareness of this? That is not the case if one postpones being in touch with it now for the sake of getting something in the future.

The thought of enlightenment can be highly inspirational and can give one rushes or gushes of energy in thinking, "I can get it." But it is just an idea and thought. Do we understand what is going on when this thought of enlightenment starts fueling desire and reaction? Can that come into simple awareness—in other words, shedding light on how we live? how we think? how we act?

WILLIAM: What do you think about death?

TONI: That is what we do: we think about death and scare ourselves. The thought that is trying to capture what-death-is is continuously thinking. It is trying to figure out what-is-death. "I" want to know about it; "I" want to have an attitude about it or a comforting thought about it. It is all thinking. Thinking that after death I may go to heaven or to hell—that is thought. Thinking I will be born again or reincarnated or live future lives—why do I think that? Is it because I am afraid of the thought of death? As long as thought is trying to capture this thing called death, it is continuously active; thought is actively thinking. But dying is not the activity of thought; dying is the ending of thought.

So, is it possible that thought ends? That there is just listening without knowing? Listening inwardly, outwardly, without reference to the "me, myself"? We want to continue as a self, and because we want to continue as a self, we are afraid of dying. So can there be dying to the thought of self? To the "me": "my image, my future, and my past"? Can there be dying to that thought? With simple awareness and simple listening? Not, "I am listening; what do I get out of it?" or, "Will I be enlightened if I listen?" That is simply a continuation of the concept of "me." Can there be an ending of the concept of "me"? That has to be found out.

Death is at the end of life. I haven't died yet. We all will die, and I'm not afraid of it. I don't know how I would feel if the airplane was hijacked and somebody was threatening me with a gun or the plane was going down. How can I tell? Sitting here right now, there is no fear of dying. My concern is not what will happen to me when this life ends. My concern is, can there be a dying to resentments and grudges? What he did or what she did to me—can we die to that? Be done with it? Maybe there was anger a moment ago. Can that anger end, be finished, and not carried over in the mind? Can we die to each moment so there is a freshness of living that is not possible if we keep carrying around everything that has happened?

I'm not concerned with what happens after death. That is idle speculation used to cover one's fear of death. I remember coming in touch with Buddhism and joining a Buddhist group. How nice it was thinking of these future places, thinking of having a better, more developed life. But what is crucial for us human beings is for us to be alive *now*. All these ideas of what will happen later or what I will become are not as important. Can we be in touch with what is true now?

WILLIAM: What about teachers who wear robes and say there are certain practices one can do to attain enlightenment?

TONI: That is what we human beings do. We are attached to things. Just because we are the teacher doesn't mean we are not attached to our system.

WILLIAM: Do you think there is any worth to certain practices that give one gradual steps to truth?

TONI: There are no gradual steps to truth.

WILLIAM: I read that truth is spontaneous, but things leading up to it are gradual.

TONI: I know the teaching that things leading up to enlightenment are worth doing: practices such as rituals, bowing, and incense burning. But these things don't lead to truth. They comfort us. They give us a feeling of refuge and belonging. We love being able to do something. We are conditioned to feel good if we are doing something, and this is what these things are very well suited for. These practices have nothing to do with understanding; they don't even shed light upon the practices themselves. One is not encouraged to question these practices, either. One has to have insight into what one is doing when performing a ritual, but performing the ritual itself doesn't shed light; it just gives inspiration or a good feeling or energy.

If we think certain practices can arouse energy, of course, they can. We can arouse energy in all kinds of ways, but why do we want to arouse energy? For what? Wanting is involved, self-centered motives and a goal are involved, in order to become something—to become enlightened, to become a better person. "I want to have this. I want to do this in order to get that," so I do things as a means to an end, which means I'm not really with them. I'm just doing them to get something else. Why do I perform the practices in the first place? Can I get to the bottom or root of what motivates my actions? What is the source of it?

Even when a person meditates, why is the person meditating? Is the person sitting in order to attain something? Is the person sitting because he or she has found out that by sitting, the system calms down, the heartbeat slows down, and the person feels a little bit more at ease, a little bit more relaxed? Well, then, if the person sits for that purpose, that is why one sits. If one sits down because one wants to find out what is going on, right now, then can the mind open up to listen to what is going on?

WILLIAM: Do you feel there is a practice that a person can do to open the mind?

TONI: No, I don't think so. If the mind opens up, it isn't due to a cause. Every teacher will tell you, "I have the Way to open up the mind. I have the means. Come into my group or tradition or church and learn the practices, and you will get what you desire: an open mind, or enlightenment." But one has to find out for oneself.

I don't know how a mind opens up. I couldn't tell you. It is either open or closed. When it is closed, we perform all kinds of practices to get it open. When it is open, we don't know how it happened! We may deduce or think this led to that. If I practice focusing my mind on certain parts of the body, it causes energy in those spots. We can do all kinds of things with practices. Things happen when we color in a coloring book. I have a grandson, and we color together. It is a very soothing thing, putting things in between lines. I once heard about a woman in a psychiatric ward. She had very erratic brain waves. They had electrodes hooked to her brain, and the brain waves became very steady while she was adding numbers, but when the sums were added and the task was over, the brain waves were erratic again.

WILLIAM: Do you feel that all religions lead to the same place?

TONI: We haven't defined what we mean by *religion*. If religion is the church and the organization, I think organization breeds division and conflict, not just among its own members but with different organizations.

I don't want to be disrespectful, but where do religions lead to? To perpetuating themselves, getting followers? Do religions lead to finding the truth? I cannot answer that. Think of all the religions that have existed and perpetuated themselves throughout history and the wars that have been fought in the name of religions—religious wars.

There are no paths in finding truth, just energy gathering to wonder, to look, and to be silent. If there is the clarity of seeing what is true, what is so, that is not Christian truth or Buddhist truth or Muslim truth. Truth has no qualities about it, no names or labels or tradition. Truth has no tradition. Tradition is man-made and woman-made. It is the product of thought and the accumulation coming out of that thought and action. Does that sound upsetting?

WILLIAM: Disturbing.

TONI: Disturbing is the right word. Don't we need to be shaken out of our molds? We just continue so happily-ever-after in what we believe, and we say that every religion leads to the same truth. These are all nice thoughts and philosophical attitudes, but what is actually happening? Let us look at what is actually happening and let go of our ideal setups! But maybe that's not exciting enough.

WILLIAM: What makes you happy in life?

TONI: That question has "me" in it and "my" happiness and "my" life—all these different elements. As long as there is this sense of me and my life and "Am I happy or not?" there is no happiness. I prefer to use the word *joy*. *Happiness* has a certain ring to it that doesn't go very deep for my personal taste. There is joy if there is walking through the woods and watching the snowmelt trickle from the branches. The little creek down the road is all frozen over, but underneath it is sputtering and gurgling. This morning the sun rose with a clear sky. Just after the moon had set, there were crows cawing from one tree to another. The beauty of it all, the stillness of it, the freshness of the morning—there's a joy in that. Or being with another human being when there is no sense of division or competition or wanting something from each other. Isn't that joy? The word doesn't capture it.

WILLIAM: What makes you sad?

TONI: When I see how little children, those so full of wonder and innocence, become conditioned to behave politely—I'm referring to the whole process of child raising, the deadness of it, the deadening of the curiosity of children. Also, the lack of love among parents, lack of love among human beings. Maybe we could say there is "evil," because there is no love; because when there is love, there is no "evil."

I get sad when we do things so compulsively yet so ignorantly, so darkly, hurting each other and hurting children without realizing what we are doing, justifying it or defending it or just ignoring it.

Sometimes anger wells up. At what? If one isn't understood

rightly, anger wells up and wants to set something right, but it doesn't last.

WILLIAM: What do you feel is the most important thing you have learned from living?

TONI: Everything is important.

WILLIAM: What was the most significant event that ever happened to you?

TONI: Coming upon the teachings of Krishnamurti ten years ago. I realized that while I thought a certain degree of freedom and insight had been attained, one really was attached—hung up on a system, a method, and spiritual advancement. One needs really to open the eyes to all that had been ignored, even though one felt well advanced in a tradition.

I could so easily put it into words and it would sound like Zen training, but it was different from Zen. Zen professes and says the same thing, but in practice, in fact, it isn't so. There are certain things that are not looked at, not examined and questioned. One doesn't question things; one continues with the whole format of it—the belief system, rituals, and ceremonies. The position of the teacher and the whole teacher-student relationship is not examined. It is sanctioned. Whatever the teacher does, bow and serve. I could go on and on. What came to mind when you asked this question was, "Don't believe, but find out. Look for yourself."

WILLIAM: Do you think a person can be truly free and still fall into traps?

TONI: The moment there is no awareness, we are in a trap. We cannot assume we have attained freedom for the rest of our life. We cannot assume anything. We have to look and be aware. When there is no awareness and there is attachment to anything, then there is no freedom.

WILLIAM: Can a person have a constant perception of truth?

TONI: That has to be found out by each person. The instant there is no awareness, something else clicks in, and that is the conditioned mind. There can be partial awareness of the conditioned mind, yet with a continuing of conditioning. If the aware-ness is full, then the conditioning leaves. If you ask, will this last forever?—find out. Why do we want this guarantee? It is theoret-ical or speculative.

WILLIAM: Are there teachers who are totally free?

TONI: Look what is happening among teachers. Very often it is explained as the teaching methods of the teacher. If there is a questioning of it, students may be told that this is their ego being judgmental of the teacher. That is one thing demanded of stu-dents by their teachers: an almost unconditional turning of one-self over to the teacher. In Zen teaching I was told the teacher sits in the Buddha's place. When I started teaching, I was told, "You are sitting in the Buddha's place." Can you imagine what happens to the mind when one is being told that, and then the students start coming and prostrating to the teacher?

WILLIAM: What made you approach life this way? Was there something that was happening that made you look for the truth?

TONI: The traumatic happenings during the years of my child-hood in Germany: the persecution of Jews; the War; the disap-pearance of people I knew and those who did not come back from the front; the air raids; the incessant news of destruction and killing; fear for one's own life, either through being taken to a concentration camp or being burned in an air-raid shelter. Just a deep questioning of what the sense of it all was. What was the sense of this senseless life? Did it make any sense? And yet, never giving up on it and always wondering about it gave me no peace. I asked the usual questions: What is the meaning of this? Why are we here? These questions were accompanied by very depress-ing feelings.

WILLIAM: Do you feel there is something life still has to teach you?

TONI: Every moment, life is teaching. I don't consider learn-ing to be stashing things away in the memory bank and accumu-lating and drawing on that. That kind of learning has its place in mathematics or making shelves. There can be learning every moment because every moment is new. The Buddha's last words were, "Be a lamp unto yourself." See for yourself; find out for yourself. Most people want advice so they don't have to look for themselves.

5

Is Mindfulness the Same as Awareness?

There is real beauty in a truly mindful person: it goes with the work, with doing something wholeheartedly, being at one without any resistance. . . . The self-conscious doer, the one expecting recognition, actually destroys wholeness. Only when attention comes out of unself-conscious doing can there be true awareness. Awareness, the way the word is used here, is not self-centered at all.

TONI PACKER: You asked yesterday whether awareness was the same as mindfulness. Shall we take that up now?

PARTICIPANT 1: Yes!

PARTICIPANT 2: Actually, I was wondering whether attention is the same as mindfulness.

TONI: Before going into this question in depth, let me say something in general about the use of words and concepts in these dialogues.

We need to be clear at the outset that most words and concepts can have interchangeable meanings. This is often an arbitrary matter. We are free to use the word *attention* in the same way that someone else might use the word *mindfulness*. Or we can agree to give the same meaning to two different words where someone else may have different meanings for each word. What is important is that we all agree on the meaning for each word and stick to that for the time being. It will avoid unnecessary arguments and confusion.

The concepts (or words) of "mindfulness" and "attention" are used here with the tacit assumption that there is somebody *doing* it—*someone* being mindful or attentive. There is the subject "I" being mindful or attentive to something or somebody. Duality is implied. For example, we received a lot of mindfulness (attention) training at the Zen center, frequently being admonished to be one with what we were doing. I felt a lot of self-consciousness in this at-oneness with walking, eating, or cleaning, sometimes looking out of the corner of my eyes to see if I was being seen as a mindful person, particularly by the teacher—wondering if it was meritorious to be a mindful (or attentive) student. Maybe I would be readily admitted to sesshin if I were found to be attentive, mindful.

And there is real beauty in a truly mindful person: it goes with the work, with doing something wholeheartedly, being at one without any resistance. But when we were occasionally told that we looked like a Buddha at such moments, it quickly resulted in self-consciousness for me—that was the end of true mindfulness and attention! The self-conscious doer, the one expecting recognition, actually destroys wholeness. Only when attention comes out of unself-conscious doing can there be true awareness. Awareness, the way the word is used here, is not self-centered at all. [*pause*]

Does somebody want to say something?

PARTICIPANT 1: I want to hear you repeat that. [*laughter from the group*] Just the last part.

TONI: There's a book out there called *The Wonder of Presence*. It has a whole chapter called "Consciousness, Attention, and Awareness" that explains the differences very carefully. But I don't mean to make a special advertisement for that book. So, what was it you wanted me to repeat?

PARTICIPANT 1: I really didn't fully hear the last couple of sentences. Maybe I was distracted. I don't know. Maybe someone else heard them and can remember . . .

PARTICIPANT 3: Was it that mindfulness can slip *into* awareness?

TONI: Only if you're not there self-consciously.

PARTICIPANT 3: . . . if you're not there?

TONI: When you're not the self-conscious "doer" of mindfulness and not the receiver of its benefits. Awareness is here spontaneously—the beauty of just the doing, totally in focus, and not blurred because I'm also thinking that *I'm* doing this well or *I* could be doing it better, or the others are more mindful than *I am*. Not wondering whether the teacher or the Buddha will be pleased with me!

PARTICIPANT 4: At that moment it's not a practice. There's the practice of mindfulness, but at that moment it's just the doing.

TONI: Yes, it's not a self-conscious practice.

PARTICIPANT 4: As a practice, it's part of separation—separation between me and what I'm doing.

TONI: That's a good distinction. On the one hand, mindfulness can be associated with the idea "I've got to practice it," and then again it comes spontaneously out of the wholeness of the situation. You cannot help being at one—it's so wholesome, so wonderful no matter what you are doing. The task changes in the light of awareness, or mindfulness in that sense—it's no longer fragmented but becomes whole and complete.

PARTICIPANT 5: For me it comes back to what we were talking about yesterday, about the scientist who is so focused on the work, that there *is* just that and nothing else. And you'll remember I asked the question about, when you're writing an article, do you hear the birds, do you hear this or that? So the mindfulness . . . we'll call it that . . . happens, the being completely absorbed, completely with what one is doing. But a lot of the time, maybe most of the time, it's like the rest of the world is shut out.

TONI: Yes, total absorption is *not* the same as awareness. In absorption there is a shutting off of everything else so one can completely pursue the one thought problem (or the carpentry work or whatever). But it doesn't have to be that way. I'm not a scientist, but even when I'm getting very absorbed in writing or in speaking, the senses remain open and interconnected. Of course—you can test me on that—I may simply not know when I'm shut off!

PARTICIPANT 6: I'm interested in this process of what I call "catching a thought." For example . . . I'm going for a walk and suddenly there's a thought pattern that has a lot of anxiety behind it. Maybe I have a business meeting coming up and the mind starts to go at it. One can catch it and see that to go with that thought pattern is only getting embroiled in a mess. And so one can maybe release it. But then there's still a sense of something lurking, something . . . it's like gnats. [group laughter] Very much like gnats. And I've been trying to be with this and see it. I try to enter in and be more present with it and not get pulled into whatever it is that seems to be lurking. Isn't that somehow connected with mindfulness? I was also thinking about that whole question of choicelessness we touched on the other day. It feels like if one doesn't go with the messy stuff, then there seems to be mindfulness in the sense of actively not going there. And yet I'm wondering if that's all trickery because of all this lurking stuff.

TONI: Not just lurking. The brain has a compulsion to solve something unfinished, to get involved. It doesn't accept letting it remain unfinished. It wants to fiddle with it.

PARTICIPANT 4: Figure it out.

TONI: Figure it out. Predict. A deep compulsion. And you can be mindful of the whole thing, but you still have to have a good meeting or speak with the people or whatever. Like the letter writer who was so upset with me, telling me he didn't want to have any more correspondence with me. Later he e-mailed back to say he appreciated my reply and to please keep up the correspondence. That interchange was the end of the disturbance;

there was no more preoccupation left for the brain once there was this mutual understanding. That finished it.

PARTICIPANT 7: Until you got that e-mail that ended the pre-occupation . . . how can one be with that preoccupation? Is there a way to be present with it?

TONI: Well, yes . . . you're not absent. I mean you're not try-ing to get away from it. Of course, when we sit in meditation, there is the energy that overrides relative concerns, but when that energy dwindles . . . there are the overriding concerns again! I think that is the only way to be with it: to enter into this *realm of meditation* right then and there. Then the whole thing feels different. It doesn't have a sting.

As you're driving to your meeting, you probably don't have the quietness and space [of this retreat] to listen quietly. So—what do you do? You are still driving. You still go into that meeting. Maybe something will happen as you talk, particularly if you talk not out of defensiveness and aggression—that tit-for-tat kind of interac-tion—but somehow manage to speak and listen more openly and dispassionately. That would help. To wonder, "Where are we all coming from?" and not project enemies who want to do "me" harm. It's not easy, because of all these trigger points that so eas-ily get activated. Which simply doesn't happen when the energy of presence is clear and strong.

6

Can Our Problems Be Figured Out?

It is a radical perception that there is absolutely nothing to gain, nothing to get, nothing to be, nothing to hold on to. As I say this, do you already notice a subtle resistance to it? Or is there simply thinking, "Yes. It's OK." Nothing to get. Nothing to be. Nothing to understand, for that matter. Being here is totally sufficient. It doesn't need to be understood.

PARTICIPANT 1: I'm wondering what causes thoughts to start back up again after they've stopped for an instant. The body relaxes, and sometimes there is a moment of unbiased, pure perception, like hearing a line of poetry and getting it instantly. But then the mind starts up again. And I wonder what causes the thinking, interpreting, separation into "me" and the birdsong (or poem) to start up again. Is a more radical seeing needed? Does that make sense? Toni, you once said that seeing is enough, that seeing *is* the change. And it seems like there's seeing for an instant, but maybe not radical enough. The mind is just relentless.

TONI PACKER: Relentless in starting up time and time again, yes. Is there also relentlessness in questioning what is really happening? "How did this start? How? Why?"

Waking up is the first thing, of course, waking up to the fact that there is renewed involvement in doubting, fear, anger, resentment, or just images of the past. "What's going on right now? And how did it happen?" Be careful to stay with the wondering, wondering with *inwardly* open eyes and ears. Is there really true wondering? Maybe the thought arises, "I don't see anything"—arousing emotions that obscure seeing. Can habitual thought be ignored and drop away so that only ongoing sensations remain without the compulsion to make anything out of them? We become so enamored of our physical sensations that we proceed to name them, think about them, and make images of them—so much unnecessary extra involvement. It's enough that sensations are there, as lightly, as sparsely, as possible. Not-knowing and not making a story out of what we feel, why we feel that way, noticing how the brain clamors to get involved in an interesting story again: "Why is this happening to me? Is it my karma? Why don't I have more clarity?" See it and drop it! Notice the resistance to dropping it, because there is a strong urge to live in continued story lines about "me"—"me" the enjoyer, the sufferer, the terrific person, or the miserable one. See it and drop whatever comes into view so that the only thing left is *just seeing*, then *dropping*, again seeing, dropping. . . . Whatever appears is seen and disappears with the seeing, coming and going, coming and going. . . .

Is this radical? What's radical is not doing anything with what appears. Let it be. Let it be. Just notice the urge to do something with it, to become somebody in the wake of what is felt right now, what is just thought about. No need to become *anything*.

PARTICIPANT 1: Do you mean even with an insight, for example?

TONI: If that's what's happening right now, yes! There's the insight. Does the thought creep up, "How marvelous, I had an insight! How can I keep it? Now I'm one of the Awakened Ones!" Drop it like poison ivy. Once you see it as poison ivy, you drop it. If you don't see the danger accurately, you want to hang on to what you found, and get some more of it to create a pretty arrangement!

PARTICIPANT 1: So don't try to hold on to anything!

TONI: Just stay with seeing. This may sound like a meager life, at least in the beginning, because we like to hold on to dreams and fantasies. But seeing clearly is our true nature. It's a totally new kind of living.

PARTICIPANT 2: If I could follow up on this . . . isn't there an involuntary quality to this? I mean, not only to the stuff that keeps coming up but also to the notion that there's something to figure out here?

TONI: Yes, yes.

PARTICIPANT 2: Over the years, I've found that my mind, especially in retreats, is just clamping down on something to figure out. This seems to go on all the time. My sleeping hours are even more disturbed than my waking hours. Sometimes I can let go of things when I'm awake, but when I'm asleep, well, it seems this mind goes on and on, trying to figure things out. I wake up exhausted.

TONI: The "figuring-out mind" trying to hold on all the time—it doesn't want to let go.

PARTICIPANT 2: It doesn't, and sometimes exhaustion and despair seem to be the best places to get to in a retreat [*laughing*], because then there may be some letting go, some chance of restful sleep. But I'm wondering, is there a way to let go without first having to get to exhaustion and despair?

TONI: You've already been there! You have seen: it can't be figured out! This becomes a deeper conviction than the assumption that it *can* be figured out. It *can't* be figured out! Problems with your job probably can be figured out. The figuring-out mind can be cultivated and rewarded, because it's fun to figure things out—engineering or math problems, for example. *But this thing of seeing the false as false and dropping it cannot be figured out.* It simply happens in the light of clear *seeing*!

I mentioned the movie that touched me so much [see chapter 23 of this book] in which a brilliant mathematician cannot *figure out* the problems created by his schizophrenic mind and ends up in total despair. Finally the realization dawns that it's impossible to figure it out—and then something else takes over. This "something else" is not persistence in ignorance and denial but awareness in the midst of despair, whatever the "flavor of the moment" may be. It won't stay. Just staying awake—awake with the deep realization that this (despair) too will pass. Nothing remains here for keeps. Just awareness, presence—but not the concept.

And not to be unkind to this mind that wants to figure things out. Just see how amazing, how deep, is this conviction that it *can* be figured out, figured out up here in the brain. That's why meditation is such an incredibly marvelous gift. We sit down and don't know what to "do." Just being quiet and awake, not-knowing. And trusting that. Not as a story to believe in but actually being here, quietly, with despair or pain or unfathomable happiness without needing any explanation for it. There may be a lot of activity in this bodymind, lots of wanting to do something or to escape the unknown. Then just listening to that activity—the music of it, or the cacophony. Let it come and also end as it will—nobody is doing it—it is self-generating.

PARTICIPANT 3: And, Toni, while listening to the cacophony of it, maybe also questioning what else is going on? What else is here besides the churning of this body and mind? Then the mind can begin to open up . . . to the calling of birds, or whatever is here.

TONI: Yes. Wondering: "Is there something else?" At that instant there is a stepping out of the story.

PARTICIPANT 3: Yes, because otherwise there is the tendency to focus on it.

TONI: Yes, not focusing on it. Letting it be. Together with the wind, pain, feeling of well-being, people moving, coughing, breathing. And not-knowing! *Not-knowing* is the salvation of the mind that wants to figure things out. Not-knowing!

PARTICIPANT 1: Can the mind come to understand that it can't . . . can it come to understand its own boundaries and limitations? Just give up, in a sense?

TONI: Yes, the brain can come to that understanding when it's reached its limit and quiets down. In some spiritual training centers there are rather violent practices where you are pushed to find a solution, pushed back and forth between enforced meditation and confrontations with the teacher. A moment may come when you simply give up. You are going nuts and give up. For some people, that's *kensho* or looking into one's true nature that doesn't shift and turn with bottomless desire but remains motionless in its very depth.

But, now, what is your motive for asking this question? Where are you coming from? If you want to find that moment again, experience it anew, and keep it for yourself, you are engaged in a futile search. Giving up cannot arise out of any conscious intention. Shortly before dying, my late husband, Kyle, kept imploring, "Tell me how to give up! I do not know how to do it." "You cannot do it. It happens on its own," I replied softly, reassuringly. It is seeing without doing, seeing without knowing. Hearing and not needing to know! If you need to catch a bus or plane, you need to know the schedule, how to get there on time. But right now we're talking about being here without needing to know. Sitting. Walking. Not-knowing. Without any deadlines. Yes, definitely, the brain can come to that state of quiet—inactive yet very active—and notice the subtle start-up of trying to figure something out. It can tell the beginning of that movement: "Here we go again!" It becomes transparent.

Transparency is already a state of quietness. Right? Detecting: "Here I go again." You feel the contraction physically—tension, stress—and also know, from past experience, that this is futile. You don't know what gets you to that quiet moment, but you know it's futile to try to get someplace. You're here already. Here. With all the . . . subtle sensations of the moment, yes?

[*long pause*]

What is the state of mind right this moment? Do thoughts say, "I don't know what she's talking about?" Or are thoughts silent? Is there a feeling of being at a loss? Or not even wanting to describe it?

PARTICIPANT 1: I'll try. It's really none of those things. The state of mind right now is listening, absorbing what you said. That's the direct answer. And there's also some agreement, some understanding, some attachment to my own experience. And yet also wondering about the experience of . . . of . . . being able to hear the call of the birds and also, at the same time, thoughts running and tension going on in a relentless kind of way. So the source of my question is seeking relief, and wondering if some more radical perception or awareness is needed.

TONI: It is a radical perception that there is absolutely nothing to gain, nothing to get, nothing to be, nothing to hold on to. As I say this, do you already notice a subtle resistance to it? Or is there simply thinking, "Yes. It's OK." Nothing to get. Nothing to be. Nothing to understand, for that matter. Being here is totally sufficient. It doesn't need to be understood.

PARTICIPANT 4: So then the problems have the same quality as the breathing, or the wind that we hear. Though normally we are fixated on a problem, and we don't see clearly that we're fixated on it. No space available. But then this can open up, including breathing, wind, rain, whatever happens. Often, though, I get stuck on a problem. And I may see that, but I'm still really focused on the problem and the openness is not there.

TONI: What sees this? Something sees this. That's what is significant. I don't mean the stuckness! Just *awaring*. *Awaring*.

PARTICIPANT 1: What's the difference between that moment of having some understanding that you're stuck, just enough space to aware that you're stuck, and now being unstuck, open? There's maybe an intellectual understanding, or even something deeper than that, and yet I could not say in any way that this has the same quality as the call of the bird.

TONI: Because the body is totally riled up?

PARTICIPANT 1: Yeah.

TONI: So give that body all the space it needs to be riled up, without expecting it to stop. No pressure whatsoever. Just falling silent in the riled-upness of the body. There may be other things going on, but this riled-up body may dominate for quite a while. It's very powerful. And it has its own powerful reactions, such as "I want to get rid of it; I don't like it; it's going to kill me."

So, be there with it! Totally you. Not as a sufferer. Not as somebody struggling with it. Nobody here. No body, no mind, no thing—not a thing, nothing.

7

Firewood Does Not Turn into Ashes

An Interview with Toni Packer
by Craig Hamilton*

It makes a big difference whether we speak and look and ask and listen from the timeless or from involvement in the changing, in time, which includes wanting things to change, wanting to change ourselves—which is all part of the changing relative world the Easterners speak of.

CRAIG HAMILTON: As humanity heads into the third millennium, the world is changing in ways that would have seemed like good science fiction only decades ago. From biotechnology to nanotechnology, from the information revolution to the deterioration of the biosphere, from globalization to global warming,

---

* Craig Hamilton, former managing editor of *What Is Enlightenment?* magazine, has moved on to pursue his independent interests in the fields of collective intelligence, the science and religion dialogue, and the social and spiritual challenges facing postmodern society today. He has recently joined the on-air team at New Dimensions Radio.

life in the twenty-first century is becoming increasingly complex, chaotic, and unpredictable. The challenge of keeping up with the speed of life has never been greater, and according to most futurists, we haven't seen the half of it. They tell us that the rate of change itself is increasing exponentially, and shows no sign of slowing down anytime soon. This recognition has led many of the most forward-looking thinkers of our time to the conclusion that in order to meet the increasing demands of life in our evolving world, new capacities are going to be required of all of us—not the least of which will be an unprecedented willingness to change and keep changing in order to respond to new life conditions as they emerge.

You are a teacher of what has traditionally been called "enlightenment"—the life-transforming realization of our ultimate nature, which is widely considered to be not only the summit of all spiritual seeking but the greatest and final aim of human existence. This profound spiritual awakening has often been described as the realization of the changeless, the timeless, the unborn, the uncreated—the absolute reality that remains forever untouched by anything that happens in the world of time, evolution, and becoming. What I would like to ask you is this: What does the discovery of this timeless dimension of being have to tell us about how to respond to the challenges of a world in which time itself seems to be accelerating out of control? How can the realization of the changeless help us to navigate a future in which constant change may well be the only constant?

Toni Packer: Right now as we are sitting here, where are we? Are we in this timeless presence without division, without "you" and "me"? Is this from where we're going to look and talk? Or are we engaged in this accelerating, changing world? Because it makes a big difference whether we speak and look and ask and listen from the timeless or from involvement in the changing, in time, which includes wanting things to change, wanting to change ourselves—which is all part of the changing relative world the Easterners speak of. This, to me, is essential. Because the time-less presence—emptiness, if you will, or wholeness—*that* does not *do* anything. That does not operate in the usual way that we are accustomed to. It just beholds, observes, listens, understands, re-alizes. Zen Master Dogen once said, "Firewood does not turn into ashes." When I heard that the first time, I didn't know what he was talking about because obviously firewood turns into ashes. I mean, we've all experienced it. So the next time I was at a camp-fire, I watched and observed, and the time quality fell away. It was just being there, and there was no change from fire to ashes; it was just what was: fire, and then sometimes it collapses, and there are some sparks, and it seems to turn black. But when you're really there, timelessly, it is not a process of time that is observed but presence: eternal, everlasting, without time.

If you are established in this timeless presence, if you are in touch with it, you don't have to navigate and negotiate. You're just here, and a response will come out of this intelligent or wise presence. One's response will be intelligent. That presence does not even perceive change as change. That's already an evaluation of what's going on. It just responds to what is here. If there is this timeless quality in one's perception, then it's not that one sees that something is changing from this to that. One simply sees what is and responds.

There cannot be any prescription for how to respond to what is going on in the world, but we are responding every moment, from moment to moment. So is there some awareness of how we're responding, what is going on in ourselves, in the world, in each other? Is there some clarity about it so that the response is appropriate?

You see, it's not that we have to become something different or go to the other shore. *We are here.* We have to wake up to that fact, and then there is a different response to what we call the rel-ative world. It's seen through for what it is. It's like when you watch a politician on television—can't you see through the face, see what the person is all about? No words are needed to realize it. If you're taking part in it—if you're taking this position or that—then you project onto the other. But the beauty is that when there's no projection, then things and people appear the way they are, unvarnished.

From this vast, unprejudiced, and nonpreferential perspective, from this presence, the relative world spins and spins according to unfathomable patterns. But this Earth is part of a huge, vast cosmos of stars exploding, and stars newly created out of hot gases. So what are we trying to do? To change this? Can we? Or is it possible just to behold wisely what goes on here and see whether it will not go out of control? The changes come and go like the tide. If war doesn't break out here, it breaks out someplace else. We haven't really changed fundamentally. But let me make it clear, I'm not pessimistic at all. On the contrary, I'm full of serenity and good cheer—not about events in the world that you're talking about as running out of control, but about this potential for a human being to wake up to what we are, changelessly.

part two

THIS "ME"
AND WHO I AM

8

About Ego

The difficulty in our relationships is that we don't see our mutual images as transparent projections, but take them personally as truth and thus keep smarting in their wake.

CAN WE START WITH distrusting *ideas* about others and ourselves the next time we feel their oppressive weight? Statements like "I'm no good at this" or "I'm too good for this" or "People don't like me—they don't talk well about me" can be questioned for their validity. "How do I know that this is true?" Questioning not only the relevance of such statements but also the soundness of the emotions and tensions that grow out of labeling each other "good" or "bad." Can we look and listen inwardly to track down this "me," this "I," every time it makes itself painfully or pleasantly felt? What is it really?

New space creates itself out of genuine curiosity, serious questioning. What is this "me" that seems so much at the center of our stories—creating conflicts, suffering, unfulfilled wanting, pleasures, and a sense of insufficiency resonating deeply within us?

Does everybody know and experience feelings of insufficiency? Very likely we all do. We are born as helpless, vulnerable creatures. Though the newborn baby is amazingly whole and complete, it can't fend for itself, and it does not "know" about itself. It's totally at the mercy of other people's feedback, gathering and embodying in a growing sense of personality ("me"-ness) whatever judgments, descriptions, and labels have been given it by others: "You're a good baby," "You're a bad boy," "You're so cute," "You are smart, talented, clumsy, lazy, angry, bright, dull." These verbal attributes build up a construct of "self" in the brain that causes alternating pleasure, pain, sorrow, and infatuated attachment. We are deeply convinced that we actually *are* these different images, aren't we?

But we are also free to question the validity of self-images. If it becomes increasingly transparent how much they dominate our thinking and reacting, space may open up to actually see them and see *through* them as sheer imagery bare of reality. Then the question arises naturally: Is *that* what I am—a buildup of images, stories—or is there something true to this "me" other than projection upon projection?

Last night during group dialogue, somebody reported feeling painfully rejected when her husband didn't happily accept the leftover soup she had offered him for supper. He just said, "I'll cook for myself." Hearing this as a participant in someone else's story, we may think, "What an unkind response!" We will remember our own experiences of "rejection" and sympathize with the person, entering into someone else's story like stepping onto slippery ice.

But first let's wonder for a moment if it is really an insult to be refused an offer of leftovers with the comment, "I'll cook for myself." Is it inevitable that one would feel rejected and hurt by that remark, with all that goes with feeling hurt? How easy living would be if we stayed off that slippery ice of vulnerable self-images!

Reactions of hurt arise from habit. There is also the tacit assumption that we *ought* to feel rejected and *ought* to show our hurt to the "offender." Then things either run their course through pouting or hurting back, or the whole reaction can be *seen* at one glance, with the liberating question "Does it really have to keep on going that way?"

The difficulty in our relationships is that we don't see our mutual images as transparent projections, but take them personally as truth and thus keep smarting in their wake: "That person doesn't appreciate me; she is moody and I can't deal with moody people. I've got to stay away from her and talk to others to find out whether they agree with me about her." We attribute things to others and to ourselves that may not be accurate at all.

No need to make matters complicated. Just to keep open the simple question whether one needs to feel rejected, or whether one can see a situation *factually* the way it is: "He doesn't want me to fix him leftover soup but rather wants to cook for himself." That's clear. Finished.

There is tremendous investment in this "I," the center of the story, longing for gratitude and love. This person herself admitted after a moment of reflection, "I was probably not intending kindness toward him at all. I was doing it for myself. Yet I wanted to be seen as a nice, thoughtful, helpful wife." Then what happens when our desire to be seen as kind and thoughtful falls flat?

Can we let go of the expectation of gratitude? How quickly can it drop? It takes a flexible, "seeing" mind to let go of a story about "me," the victim. Story making is one of the most favorite occupations of the brain, but it needn't become emotionally entangling. Awareness need not be clouded by emotional reactions. When self-centered (emotional) stuff is left out of the picture, our relationships become easier and lighter.

All of us walk around wrapped in all kinds of changing moods that are woven out of thinking about "who knows what about me." Just like the weather that doesn't have much stability, our moods change all the time depending on whether we assume people are thinking well of us or not. Recollecting that someone disliked me creates an immediate mental burden, just as remembering someone's approving remarks or smile frees up the burden.

Can we live around a person who is temporarily under the cloud of moodiness and not take it personally? Without getting annoyed by it? Or do thoughts immediately start spinning: "He should not talk like that, not treat me that way. It clearly shows that he doesn't like me." "I'm not worthy of being loved." Just see all these ideas stirring around like drifting clouds. Why take them personally? Just let them be seen the way they are drifting in this moment. Can we agree that taking it easier with our temporary moods makes them dissipate faster? They need not be justified or defended! We help each other greatly by accepting each other's moodiness, letting it be a passing mind-state that we know we're all burdened with at one time or another. When the sun appears from behind the cloud cover, how liberating is the effect upon our moods!

9

Am I My Body?

We can wisely admonish others and ourselves: "Don't be identified with your body." But what does that mean? Try not to settle superficially for the words but ask what they really point to, so that we can understand each other more deeply.

IT'S A DAY HEAVY with clouds and humidity. You feel it as you walk through the meadows, wetness penetrating shoes and socks—you feel wet and cold on your toes. Grasses sparkle with moisture, with translucent droplets of pearl. These grasses! It never tires to look at them, all the varied colors and shapes and their graceful movements in the wind.

Today I walked down into the lower meadow, the tops of blades full with yellow seeds. Some were tall enough to touch the clouds! Couldn't go far since the feet were hurting badly—I had to limp along the mowed path, feeling a bit foolish. I'm saying this so you need not ask me, "What's the matter with your feet?" Right now they are happily resting on a stool—burning, yet thankful for the cooling air. Discomfort is passing. That's the amazing thing about all the different states of bodymind: They pass. They come, they go. Some of them linger, but they will change eventually. The art of living is not to make stories about any of them, because stories linger longer than the states they're describing. Much longer. For centuries sometimes.

People often affirm what we read in traditional texts from the East: "I am not my body." "You are not your body!" It can be beneficial to use those words like a mantra worth repeating when one is strongly identified with "my" hurting body, painfully worried about it. It can be helpful when a set of fresh words replaces worn-out, depressing phrases.

Does it bring about some relief to hear, "You're not your body"? Up to a point, yes. But it only goes so far, since a voice immediately replies, "It does feel that *I* am my body! These are '*my*' aching feet, not *yours*. It definitely feels that *I* am the owner of this body, no one else."

So, then, what do we mean by this "I," and what about this ownership? Are we willing to inquire deeply into this? Watching the state of mind, the effect of the words upon the organism when we say, "*I* am in pain," "It's *my* body," "You're hurting *me*," or when we (deliberately at first) leave out these powerful words and simply describe what is going on? Like "Right now there is pain in the feet," or "It really hurts when you say those words."

We can wisely admonish others and ourselves: "Don't be identified with your body." But what does that mean? Try not to settle superficially for the words but ask what they really point to, so that we can understand each other more deeply. Don't just accept what Toni is saying. Question it. We can question together. Then the one who says things is invited to look, and to speak out of that depth of looking.

What does it mean to be identified with this body? Does it mean that it is the most essential part of my story? We can hear that story when we listen inwardly, let what goes on in thought become transparent. This story about me and my body is as long and as old as I am, and it's taken for a true representation of what I am.

Is that what *identification* means? An integral part of this story is the "me," believed to be (in) this body. If you ask me, "What are you or who are you?" I can give you my name and instantly point to this body, saying, "This is me."

I remember going through all this many years ago, racking my brain about this "I" and "me," trying to get to the root of it while driving to Rochester on the interstate. And if you, too, are interested in finding this out, go quietly into it any time it comes up for you. It is amazing to experience this quandary, this wondering, and investigating into not-knowing, because it really seems to exercise the brain and allow it to move outside its accustomed pathways of talking and thinking. Questioning can shake it up, loosen its stuckness. Like we've said before, "cracking the cement of language."

So when I say I am not my body, does it mean it's no longer part of this picture story? This story has ended, maybe just for a moment, for the time being. A moment here doesn't mean measured time—it simply means seamless space of awareness.

So, for a moment *not* thinking in words about me and my body, its past and its future—does that open up free space? Try it, find out. Or maybe it's just an exercise in deliberately speaking differently, which is all right too. It's still a good exercise not to think and talk in words about "me and my body." But then maybe for an instant there is a true opening—the habitual routine is gone and there are just birds twittering and the fan humming, a voice producing words, body vibrating with sound, muscles flexing gently, breathing in and out—all of that right here fleetingly filling open space. And as you walk through the glistening meadow, here are the tall grasses and the clouds, the beauty of every single sparkling blade. What amazing works of art each single one of them is—tall and slender, with yellow seedpods delicately waving in the breeze.

Does the mind come in and say, "Now I understand what it means, I am not my body—I am the whole," or whatever words have been said about it? Does thought say, "I am that, I am this?" Alan Watts wrote a book that I gobbled up—its title is *The Supreme Identity*. It provided some marvelous new words. I'm not saying the author didn't know what he was talking about. But the reader—what happens to us? The brain in its attachment to security is constantly searching for concepts to attach to that which is beyond all words, all concepts and ownership.

It's an elating feeling to think, "Now I've shed my ego identity because I know I'm the supreme identity!" I went through that elated feeling, quite unawares. But readers, beware! Isn't it the task of the author of books to keep the written work lucid but loose, open, unfixed, flexible, to keep reminding the reader that the word is not the real thing and can be substituted by another word any time? Isn't it the author's task to sustain the reader's curiosity to find out *what is the real thing*, abiding nowhere? Is curiosity alive this moment?

Krishnamurti never tired of saying, "The word is not the thing." Do we understand that? Even though words are used? There wouldn't be talks or articles if there weren't words used as conveyors. For one thing, more is conveyed in a talk than just the words. Are we together in the depth of words and beyond the words? Can words point beyond themselves?

The total energy of presence allows the mind to see what the word merely points to. To see it here, within myself. Not out there, but here. To feel the shift from "out there" to "right here." The shift from being in a tunnel of wordy "me"-ness to . . . inexpressible openness. Do you see? Is it happening right now? Here? Now?

So, did we say enough about identity, the story of "me" as this body, or "me" as "not this body," "the supreme identity"? When this experience of "openness" happens, . . . it's not really an experience. This openness, this presence, this nondivision, is not an "experience." Because there is no one here who experiences it through thinking, even though the body's heart is beating, the breath is flowing; the feet feel refreshing cool air. As this happens, there is no story. No identity. That comes in later, with the mind that wants to explain, to conceptualize, and to possess. It's helpful, and even beautiful, to conceptualize, if one knows what one is doing and doesn't dwell in the concepts but just communicates.

Remember that the main part of communicating is being here, not the words you have found. The words are secondary. The prime, essential thing is to be here. And does that communicate? Does it? Are we here together with the birds, the fan, the body tensing or relaxing, the breath flowing?

10

Being Oneself

What I'm describing is a state of being in which one is not caught up in the need to fulfill or be some image.

PARTICIPANT 1: What do you mean, Toni, when you talk about being oneself . . . you said earlier that you now fully understood what it means to be oneself. . . .

TONI PACKER: Do you want to say more, or—

PARTICIPANT 1: No, no, I want to hear.

TONI: Let me first say what I don't mean. I don't mean in any shape or manner that there is something to be, some kind of a self, an ideal self. That's not what it is to be oneself. And that may be what's confusing, because you think, "Well, how should I be to be myself?" That's a wrong path. It is just . . . no image of oneself. Not as an ideal; it just happens. There is no image of oneself, so all of a sudden there is experienced a tremendous flow of freedom, to be alone or in relationship. Also a lovingness comes with this absence of images. But if you think, "Oh, to be oneself means to be loving, so I have to be loving," that's not it. Because if you're feeling hateful at the moment, or angry, then it's vital to see that and not try to paint it over.

So, now do I mean that if you're very angry, you should express that anger at someone else? That's an important part of that question, right? "I feel very angry, this is what I am right now"—so do

I think I should be expressing this? Well, I trust what we could call "the censor," seeing that to express this anger at this person right now would not be helpful. Not helpful. That is seen. And the anger is also seen. And there's nothing wrong with being angry. There may even be a good reason for the anger. But right then, to throw one's anger into the situation will not help. If that's clear, the anger will not express itself at that person but will be seen without condemnation.

PARTICIPANT 1: Not condemned and not carried out.

TONI: Yes. I call that action, the seeing of it. The presence with it is the action, not necessarily the expression of it.

PARTICIPANT 1: You know, when [Participant 2] was talking, and I began to feel some hurt, and there were some fears, and feeling like a child. It felt so real. I could see my body contracting and my heart pounding.

TONI: All aspects of hurt and fear, yes. But fill it in a bit. You mean hurt at the memory of the scenario or situation?

PARTICIPANT 1: Yes. The whole scenario. And the sadness of it all.

TONI: The sadness that this should be in your life, huh?

PARTICIPANT 1: Or just the sadness of the situation itself in which there could be friendliness but that is not happening at the moment, and then the anger comes and that makes it worse, and then feeling hurt comes.

TONI: But does what you just described . . . seeing that it produced more pain, and the sadness of it, is that connected with repression or a condemnation of how you feel right now? Do you feel not up to par, not living up to your image of yourself, your image of how you should be, to yourself or to others?

PARTICIPANT 1: Yes, yes, I was getting in touch with that. That's where the question came from: How can we be ourselves? At that moment that the hurt came, I could feel the image of the victim wanting to take over, the victim that I have played for ages, at least that's how it feels. So I could see that, and could stay with that, and then, in the seeing, that victim story began to stop running. Though it ran for a while, that story, while the tears came.

Toni: I can see a possibility of a confusion in this "being oneself."

Participant 1: OK.

Toni: What I was describing—when I said earlier that I fully understood what it means to be oneself—was experiential, not thought about from the outside. Rather, simply realizing there was no obstacle, no barrier, and no being hemmed in to say what was going on. The flow of saying things, communicating, when something comes up and beckons to be examined, looked at—stepping in and illuminating, clarifying, wondering, and the freedom to do that, not being leery about it and worrying if this will hurt the person further or whatever, because saying something seemed the right thing to do, in a free way. So this is what I meant by being oneself. But we don't always feel this way.

Participant 1: No, those moments are, for myself, very extraordinary.

Toni: And then to guard against remembering what Toni said, and thinking, "Well, I'm really not myself, how can I be myself?" and this becoming an ideal or goal.

Participant 1: That can be dangerous.

Toni: Or bursting out and not holding back, maybe doing some harm or hurt by making angry remarks. You could say, "Well, that's also myself." But what I'm describing is a state of being in which one is not caught up in the need to fulfill or be some image. When we're caught up in imagery, meaning that we don't want to be or to be seen this way . . . can we see that, behold it? So, then what is this being oneself? Beholding it all, beholding what's in there. Maybe not feeling open, not feeling kind. But seeing it. Beholding it.

Participant 1: Yes. Beholding it. I understand. So . . . in that embrace, things can come and go.

TONI: Come and go. Not remain stagnant, not when there is this seeing lighting it all up.

PARTICIPANT 1: So tears can come, the story can run; it's all happening.

TONI: And see the thought coming up that "this stuff shouldn't be coming up because I'm a spiritual person, a developed person; I should do better than this."

11

Loneliness

We mistakenly feel that our story is our true home, and when it is not present, there is the sad feeling of missing something. Let's be careful not to linger with the sadness of loss and loneliness—not to make that part of our story. Simply *feel* it in the body and leave it alone—staying with open listening and wondering. Wondering is a marvelous antidote to the suffering of loneliness!

PARTICIPANT: I'd like to talk a bit about loneliness related to seeing one's life as a movie. In my own experience, when I start seeing my life as a dream or movie, it brings with it a different type of loneliness than just the everyday loneliness. It's something that goes all the way to the bone.

TONI PACKER: To the bone. Yes.

PARTICIPANT: There's some sort of tremendous resistance to that, a great fear that something is being lost when we do that.

TONI: When we see our life as a movie.

PARTICIPANT: Yeah.

TONI: As having a quality of unreality.

PARTICIPANT: Right. There's some sense that one starts to see the world as being of one's own making, enclosed in one's own concepts. It's like one is completely alone, maybe not really contacting anything genuinely. . . .

Toni: Not really contacting anything in a genuine, real way. But where does that "sense" come from? From a thought, a mental evaluation like "Maybe I'm not genuinely contacting things, I'm not in touch with reality, I'm locked into my own creation!" Is that what is going on? Reflections like these can create feelings of loneliness, despair, depression, or whatever mood may accompany them.

Maybe it's true that we *are* locked in mental creations! But words and concepts used to describe experiences are *not* the real thing, even though they create palpable moods.

When someone says, "See the world as a movie," it means, "See and understand 'the world' as the content of a mental story." The "I" plays an enormously important part in all our stories. It is the central doer and owner—the one who wins and loses, enjoys and suffers!

But in the midst of the story there can also be a sudden coming to—a fresh wondering if there can be a different way of being here, of listening, looking, and doing things that does not arise out of a story-world created by self-centered thinking.

So the new question is, "Is there a 'world' that is not created by the story-creating mind?" When the story-creating mind lets up, everything turns out to be very simple—just birds calling, cool fog touching the eyes, the skin, and the warmth in this room full of people. Whatever is experienced directly, wholly, is not a creation of the mind. It's what's right here without thought entanglement, without evaluation. Just rain dripping on the wooden deck—drip, drip, drip. Breathing in and out, in and out, body expanding, contracting, energy throbbing throughout the body—every moment a miracle without the interference of thoughts!

So in this "mood of loneliness"—you described it quite well in saying "it feels as though something is being lost"—well, maybe what's lost is the *illusion* that I've been in touch with what's real! Now you suddenly see it was an illusion! But thought keeps moaning, "I've lost something! How sad!" But you haven't lost anything real! That's just an idea!

[*pause*]

[*Cheep, chee chee*] Do we hear birds cheeping outside the open windows and doors? Are we right here?

[*pause*]

We feel rewarded when we live in our story, our apparent home where we feel somewhat at ease. We may not feel *safe*—human beings don't feel safe most of the time, because of a constant undercurrent of tricky thought-scenarios of past and future. And yet we habitually assume there's more safety living in our familiar thought-spun story than in a world spontaneously unfolding from moment to moment.

PARTICIPANT: I guess I'm feeling that even when I'm not so much in the story, when I'm not playing that game. What takes me back into the story again and again is this loneliness that's here even when I feel that the story isn't.

TONI: Even when the story isn't here? Well, then, is that feeling of "loneliness" due to mentally reflecting about the state of no-story? Is it like a withdrawal from the rewards of the "me"-story, the physical craving that comes out of needing that stimulation? We've been habituated to story. So when you say, "Right now I'm living in very little story, but I still feel lonely," . . . is that because it's not the habitual story-state of constant stimulation and reward? But not to stop with any thought-created conclusion and its moods, but to discover for oneself the richness of being in touch with breathing, birds calling, looking and listening freely *without any story!*

We mistakenly feel that our story is our true home, and when it is not present, there is the sad feeling of missing something. Let's be careful not to linger with the sadness of loss and loneliness— not to make that part of our story. Simply *feel* it in the body and leave it alone—staying with open listening and wondering.

Wondering is a marvelous antidote to the suffering of loneliness! Wondering: "What is right now?" Shifting from the passively enduring to actively wondering, questioning, "What is it?" Because now the senses are wide awake, listening in open wondering! Energy is flowing freely, abundantly! [*pause*] Does that make sense?

PARTICIPANT: Yes.

TONI: When things are put into words, it may sound complicated. But it isn't. It's very simple. Not easy, but simple.

[*They sit quietly for a few minutes.*]

TONI: To come back . . . we didn't go into the feeling of loneliness itself, whether it's habitual loneliness or the feeling of having lost something. You mentioned these two different kinds at the beginning. But regardless of what kind, is there a feeling, a state of mind, that is disagreeable, that causes some kind of anxiety? And how to be with that?

We looked at what brings it about, and sometimes that exploration can dispel the disagreeable state of mind because one understands how it's grounded in illusion, in just wanting the story back. But maybe disagreeableness doesn't go away. The feeling of loneliness lingers, and one discovers more and more thoughts that bring it about. Discovering those thoughts may not do away with the whole process of feeling loneliness or any other bothersome mood or unpleasant state of mind. Our life of thinking and remembering is so constituted that these states come and go all the time. There's no such thing as permanent happiness or constant equilibrium. Things of this world keep moving into and out of balance without abiding anywhere.

So is there a totally new way of letting all of that happen, be it loneliness, fear, or whatever—not bothering with it at all? To live like a water skimmer crisscrossing the water, barely touching it, not getting bogged down in wetness. No hassling with the water, no complaining about splashing and splattering.

Can we just let it be—whatever unpleasantness, discomfort, or outright pain there may be—not trying to clothe it in words, not verbalizing yet *not* denying it? The feeling isn't denied. It's there. But it's not made into anything more than it is. Whenever the urge comes up to make something out of it, see it and dismiss it. Let it go.

So just living with rainy days, hot humid days, and mellow spring nights—you're just here with it all without making anything out of it or wanting more or less of it.

Then you may notice all of a sudden that feelings of loneliness are gone. "Me" and "the world" are seen as mere words that bring about painful feelings of separation and loneliness. The feelings will return at the moment of inattention, but—so what? Just see it afresh! There is just skimming across the waters without getting wet—beholding it all without denial or acceptance of what has already passed.

12

Expectation

To say "have no expectations" is already jumping the gun. Can there be awareness of expectation right now? Listening to its buzzing? Listen to that. See that. The fundamental changes that happen to us don't happen through intention or willpower, but through simple awareness. It's almost like magic . . . if you're *truly* aware and not just using the concept of awareness.

TONI PACKER: Anyone else want to say something? A few people have been doing most of the talking so far. There's still time.

PARTICIPANT 1: I'd like to respond to the story you [Participant 5] told yesterday. It interested me, I think, because . . . well, this notion of doing things without expectations comes up a lot in this work and . . . your comments got me thinking about what the word means in a literal sense and psychological sense and . . . many senses. In one sense, expectation has a time factor. You know, you remove time present and you operate in time future, with an outcome in mind. In fact, it's scripted. You've scripted how something is going to turn out. I'm not saying that's bad. But it's a real challenge of this work . . . to resist the pull of expectation, of living in the future. To take it one step further: that kind of living in the future is also a form of fantasizing and wish fulfillment. I don't know . . . what observers say about this type of expectation is that it keeps you from living in the present. So . . . I'm asking . . . having expectation, what does it mean and how do you deal with it?

TONI: First, you notice it. That's the crucial thing. To say "have no expectations" is already jumping the gun. Can there be awareness of expectation right now? Listening to its buzzing? Listen to that. See that. The fundamental changes that happen to us don't happen through intention or willpower, but through simple awareness. It's almost like magic . . . if you're *truly* aware and not just using the concept of awareness.

PARTICIPANT 2: Sometimes it seems to me as if I'm looking at some problem or situation and that I can see what's needed to make it work better in the future. But what I overlook is that in forming the solution I'm usually doing the same thing as what the problem was. Like in trying to get rid of expectation . . . you know . . . you're floating an expectation that you'll get rid of expectation. It's so hard to intellectually look at something and see the *whole* thing because . . . does that make sense?

PARTICIPANT 1: Say more.

PARTICIPANT 2: Because . . . you don't see that what's going on is an intellectual process.

TONI: Because of thinking.

PARTICIPANT 2: Yeah, yeah. It's like a catch-22.

PARTICIPANT 3: I find that very helpful, actually, and also . . . Toni, when you talked about combating one self-image with another self-image, it occurred to me that it can be very difficult to detect that new self-image, to see that it's another image.

TONI: Because the mind is already under the landslide of this new image and what it does. It takes moment-to-moment stopping and listening. If that doesn't happen, we run with the image, the thoughts and expectations, the fears.

PARTICIPANT 3: I'm . . . I'm interested in the different ways people talk about catching that. Sometimes we talk about slowing down, stopping. Other times we say there's a sense of space opening up, catching the whole . . . uh—

TONI: —which doesn't happen unless there's a stopping of what has been running. But I didn't want to interrupt you. . . .

PARTICIPANT 3: No, no . . . so that's what I'm wondering . . . whether these are all different modes or connected or . . .

TONI: See, what you're doing now is—

PARTICIPANT 3: Yeah, combing over it and trying to make some sense of it—

TONI: —up here [*points to head*]. Isn't a better way, when a word is used and it doesn't make sense, to ask, "Well, what do you mean by that?" Right in the moment when the confusion is first there.

PARTICIPANT 3: Uh-huh. [*pause*] So then let's go back to [Participant 2] talking about seeing the whole thing. I mean, I think I know what you're getting at, but I'm not sure. Can you say any more, [Participant 2]?

PARTICIPANT 2: Yeah. Um . . . well, [Participant 1] was talking about expectation. He was saying we get into trouble when we have expectations. We hear that and our response is to try to not have expectations, to do something different . . . but . . . yes, that happens, but on its own. It's not something you can do, have control over. So I guess I was giving an example from my own experience where I tried to change what was happening. I tried to see that expectations are a problem and then I tried not to have any . . . and then somewhere down the road . . . Ah! It struck me: "That's an expectation itself!" Who knows how that happens? That consciousness that says, "Oh, that's an expectation itself!" . . . that's different than that other thing that says it's going to try to have no expectations. Does that make sense?

PARTICIPANT 1: I think that's a good point. Toni, what you're saying is . . . don't make a moral judgment that expectations are either good or bad. Just be aware that they are happening.

TONI: See it. See them. See them.

PARTICIPANT 4: Expectations can arise and go. Come and go and be seen . . . no problem, if they're not identified with, if they don't become my script.

PARTICIPANT 3: And . . . occasionally useful?

PARTICIPANT 4: Occasionally useful?

PARTICIPANT 5: Well, if you're going to Alaska and you expect it will rain, then you take the proper clothing. I don't know . . .

PARTICIPANT 6: It depends on what we mean by *expectations*. Much of what we do has a hidden story going that is full of expectations. It may not be absolutely clear. On the other hand, if we're going on a trip, it makes sense to talk to people and get information so we can do some good planning. There's nothing wrong with doing some good planning. But that's different from what we were talking about. In planning, the expectations are clearly there, they're part of the planning; in the other case they weren't being seen.

TONI: Physiologically, when there are expectations in the mind, the body is geared up toward something. A shift can happen from *thinking* more about it to a response that comes out of awareness. [*pause*] That's what you were trying to get at there, the shift from the fragmentation—which is thinking about something—to seeing the whole . . . to this awareness that is whole, wholesome.

PARTICIPANT 6: So there is more energy of presence than of expectation . . . so that, yes, you call the plumber and the assumption is that he'll be able to deal with the plumbing problem. But you have to actually watch and see what happens. . . .

TONI: Of course, there's a difference between our daily life and here in retreat, between getting a plumber or . . . retreating right now. It's harder to trace the buzz of expectation when you have to deal with the plumbing problem. So we have to discern the difference between our daily life—expecting to go someplace, you have to make reservations, or what have you—and sitting here with the sound of the fans. Right now, this body and mind are free of expectation. There may also be all kinds of things coming up—anticipation, projection—but that doesn't mean there can't also be some awareness. With daily, mundane expectations, there can be awareness, too.

PARTICIPANT 6: There's a difference between mundane expectations and those expectations that center on this idea of "me."

TONI: Yes. Like: "If I don't get the job, what a mess this will be, what will happen to me?" And there's a deep expectation of ourselves to be good. I looked at this yesterday after our discussion and this is *so* deep. Such pressure of expectation to do good, to be perfect, to have things in order. It's so deeply in our conditioning that if it doesn't turn out that way, then our whole existence seems wrecked. [*pause*] This comes back to what we were talking about earlier. We tell ourselves "Nothing is changing; it's the same old stuff. . . ." "Why am I still getting rattled, this shouldn't be happening, I've meditated all these years." Expectation. All of it. Marvel and be in awe of it all, and how this is part of the fabric of our existence, the fabric of ourselves. How are you going to change that? Change the stitches? It's still fabric. Or . . . here . . . listen . . . the hum of the wind in the leaves—and that's not an escape. That's here now. There's no pattern to that listening. No worry that "they" will dislike me for what I say, or like me. That's not there.

[*long pause*]

TONI: [*continuing*] So it's not the "opening" or "stopping"—it's none of that. It's being here. Being here and not off in self-concerned, anxiety-conditioned thought. It's not expanding oneself, expanding our consciousness. It's here! Uncontracted and unexpanded. [*pause*] Su-weet. Su-weet. [*A bird is calling outside.*]

13

My Identity

It is for you to begin to observe some of this if you can—it takes a bit of meditative presence to be with what is—just as it is—without being distracted by all the evaluations and comments that habitually arise *about* our situation. We suffer more from our stories than from the actual situation as it is.

DEAR _____,

You write, "I feel as if I have given up who I am to care for [my child]."

Who are you?

The aches, pains, and frustrations that lead us into desperation spring from being without our accustomed identities when we find ourselves at home with a child—your identities being a therapist, one with two master's degrees, a helper of people, an author, and so forth. We mistakenly think we *are* all those things, but this is only because we have never questioned and examined in depth what we truly are without any of our identities. That is meditative work. In observing ourselves honestly, we find that we are really in love with the images we have developed about ourselves (we are either in love with them or we hate them), and when they don't fit into our changed situation any longer, it feels like partial death—like losing a loved one to whom one was deeply attached. Can you examine all this carefully for yourself?

In your present state of mourning the loss of your accustomed work and identity you cannot really be with your child in an open, interested, truly connected way, can you? You cannot see her when your vision is blinded with self-absorption—with the story lines constantly running through your head about how things were, what you have given up, with all the connected emotions of grief and frustrations that go with them. Then what could be a source of delight (the unfolding of a small child, the growing up together) becomes a source of frustration, maybe anger or whatever. It is for you to begin to observe some of this if you can—it takes a bit of meditative presence to be with what is—just as it is—without being distracted by all the evaluations and comments that habitually arise *about* our situation. We suffer more from our stories than from the actual situation as it is.

Not that being with a child is always delightful—it isn't! I know that from my own experience. But without the constantly nagging thoughts, for instance that she "has taken from me what I was," and the self-pity involved in it—without that it becomes a precious opportunity to find out about ourselves and each other and life together in a new way. Not how it *could* be or how it *was* or *should* be, but how it actually is from moment to moment as we become more wakeful, less dreamy and story-ridden about our life.

Best wishes,
Toni Packer

14

About Creativity

Today I understand much better that feelings of separation between you and me disappear when our small minds of ego open up to a clear perception without the distortions created by the active "me"-network.

A FRIEND COMPLAINED about having done nothing creative in his life—nothing of enduring value in his daily work, nothing deeply satisfying, or even helpful to others.

What does it mean to be creative?

One definition is bringing something into existence that is new, original—not an imitation of anything else. It's an interesting fact that the painter, composer, sculptor, or architect are generally revered as creative individuals who are out of the ordinary. Why? Is it because great works of art are usually sold at high prices, especially after the individual has passed away? Or is it because we imagine that art arises out of pure seeing, pure listening—an uncorrupted imagination where self-enclosing thoughts do not contaminate the work? I don't know whether this is the reason. There seems to be something traditional, and therefore habitual, in feeling that the creative artist is someone special—that painting, writing, sculpting, or composing are prime examples of creation.

During his dialogues Krishnamurti passionately asked the audience around him, "Can we create something together?" In the beginning I wondered what he could mean by this "creating something together." Today I understand much better that feelings of separation between you and me disappear when our small minds of ego open up to a clear perception without the distortions created by the active "me"-network. When that's in abeyance, the free expressions of true being—compassionate interest and understanding for one another—move effortlessly without our feeling we have to habitually defend our territory and self-image.

What is there to separate us? Whatever we may do or say at times of nonseparation *is* creating something together, isn't it? In speaking or writing out of undefended openness, there's no reciting from memory (even though language depends on memory) and no ownership of what we say or do with our words.

I remember Krishnamurti questioning aloud whether baking bread was a creative act, as New Age people were frequently asserting. Hearing this question raised, can the mind refrain from immediately answering yes or no, and instead join in wondering what is meant by a "creative" act?

Have you actually ever baked bread? If you haven't but want to try it, can self-doubt give way to simply measuring out ingredients, stirring flour, water, oil, salt, and honey together, one after another, attentively, until the bare hands take over the task of mixing the heavy dough in rhythmic motions?

There is nothing more miraculous than thorough attention, no matter what the activity may be: The beauty of each movement inseparably one with the fully open senses—the watching eyes, listening ears, inhaling nose, sensitive skin, and eager taste buds—each breath taking in the fragrances of the different ingredients as they merge into a warm, bubbly ball. It invites kneading, and then letting it rise, then punching it down, and then letting it rise, then punching it down again, and finally separating the big ball into small loaves—all in easy succession. A whole life story in one loaf of bread!

Are we *here*?

I do not need to know whether this is a "creative process" or not, but I do know that it's not necessarily happening in order to become someone important. Attention includes careful awaring of the many different thoughts going on in the brain. No extraneous thinking is needed for baking bread—distractions, when seen, cease in the seeing. People want to eat freshly baked bread, so let's do it. Grease the pans, dust them with small sprinklings of flour, and lower the punched loaves into them. Let the dough rise until it towers over the pans, then place the pans into the preheated oven. What comes out at the sound of the bell is not the same as what went in!

At the Springwater Center we bake all the bread for the retreatants, and the fragrance wafting throughout the house in the mornings is delicious beyond description.

Reading these paragraphs now, quietly, effortlessly, letting the energy of words and images flow freely, are we creating something together?

15

Who Decides?

Don't carry away a conclusion unless it has been arrived at through your own experience. Rather, if there hasn't been direct experience, carry away the question.

A QUESTION LEFT from the small group meeting yesterday concerns decision making. A retreatant felt the issue wasn't quite resolved in her mind. To her, it definitely appears that "I made a decision when I decided to come here, sent my application for retreat, and yet you, Toni, say there is not really a decision maker!"

When you have these doubts, let it be a motivation for wondering and watching, which is sometimes not easy to do on one's own. It seems that when one questions by oneself, unless there is a developed capacity to do that, the energy of the wondering doesn't gather but dissipates. It is easier in a circle like this, where people sit in silence to wonder and to look together.

So let's go into this. Let's say I have to make a decision whether to apply for a new job. Do I apply for the new job or don't I? "I have to make a decision," says the mind from old habit. The way we talk and express things is usually habitual. And any habitual expression has quite a strong power over our thinking. For example, when I finally send the application, thought says, "I have decided." Actually, quite accurately stated, a decision has been made to send the application. Whether there is an "I" that makes decisions is open to questioning. Who or what *is* that decision maker, that chooser?

A question like this may already fall into an established groove for the listener/reader: "Ah, there is Toni again with her 'Who is doing it?'" That kind of habitual reaction blocks a fresh inquiry. And it is important to approach this freshly: "How did this decision really happen?" Watch the whole process! What is really going on right now?

What is observed in the mind is the picturing of this new job—sitting at a new desk with a new boss and coworkers, more money, maybe closer to home, and so on. And the job you have at present has these and these and these attractions, but also great disadvantages—this and this and this—and you imagine it and think about it. Then thought shifts back to imagining the new job and all of its advantages, which may appear rosier every time there is a shift. Then thought shifts back to picturing the present situation, which may become less rosy with time. (It can also proceed the other way around.)

Perhaps neither of these thought-trains has sufficient weight to "win out." But usually one of them is stronger. Maybe another thought-train is added that makes it weightier, such as "It will be good to have made a decision, because then I'll be rid of this conflict." Or, "People will think I'm forever vacillating, whereas I want to be perceived as strong and decisive." The image of being a vacillator is not wanted. So you sit down and write the application, put it in the envelope, address it, stamp it, and put it in the mailbox.

If you really are interested in watching this whole process, some energy starts gathering in watching, and you may notice that finally this thing happens—the writing, or, in another case, getting up out of bed. It usually happens without a specific thought such as, "OK, now I am deciding to get up," or "I have decided to get out of bed." Thought isn't there, but all of a sudden you find yourself just writing or getting up, and then in retrospect you tell someone else, "Oh, *I* decided to finally get up," or "*I* decided to apply for this job." But if attention remains without gaps, staying strong and focused, you realize that in truth there are many trains of thought and images moving in different directions. Finally something happens, no longer clouded by thought—thought has fallen away. Later it comes back in, just as it did before. So these discoveries make you say that there isn't really a decider, only thoughts masquerading as an "I."

But don't just accept this and carry away the idea that Toni says, "There is no decision, no choice, no decider." Then you just carry away confusion, because thought will also say, "This doesn't make sense, because *I* am making a choice! *I* just made a choice to come to the center to meditate." Don't carry away a conclusion unless it has been arrived at through your own experience. Rather, if there hasn't been direct experience, carry away the question "Is Toni right? Because it doesn't make sense; it doesn't jibe with my daily observations." You may find to your surprise that what you have in mind does not really come from direct daily observations but from daily ways of talking to yourself about yourself, such as "I've made a decision," or "I have to make a choice."

What is wonderful is to carry away not any conclusions but the wondering—this wondering that generates energy to observe and listen in a totally fresh way!

part three

THIS WAR AND PEACE
BETWEEN US

16

Love and Attachment: Is Attachment Inevitable?

Do you have a hard time with the concept of the "inevitability" of attachment because you have the idea—maybe from Buddhist teachings—that you can live with somebody intimately, enjoying companionship, sex, walking together, or sharing a good meal, and still remain unattached?

PARTICIPANT: There is something left in my mind from the last retreat that hasn't been understood.

TONI PACKER: Yes?

PARTICIPANT: It's about the last talk of the retreat, when you were talking about the loss of Kyle [Toni's husband] and about your attachment to him. You said that attachment was inevitable . . . and I was wondering about that, you know?

TONI: Yes. Yes. It would be good to look deeper into that. Maybe I spoke incompletely, because, pausing and wondering deeply *right now*, attachment is *not* inevitable! But if no attachment is formed in a close relationship, there also may not be this complete communion in living and sharing together all the joyful, beautiful things, and also the hard, difficult times.

Right now shall we look into the evolving of close relationship?

PARTICIPANT: Yes.

TONI: Something grows between two people in close relationship, and when that relationship comes to an end, I have likened that experience to an amputation. A palpable energy field has developed between two people over many years, and that field is ruptured when one of the partners departs. What is left is the experience of a vacant black hole—an abandoned space—and yet the body remembers intimately what was there before, wanting it desperately while unable to get it back. That is pain and suffering. [*pause*]

So do you have a hard time with the concept of the "inevitability" of attachment because you have the idea—maybe from Buddhist teachings—that you can live with somebody intimately, enjoying companionship, sex, walking together, or sharing a good meal, and still remain unattached?

PARTICIPANT: Or . . . of course, the attachment you are talking about is not this deep kind of attachment.

TONI: Deep attachment develops in time.

PARTICIPANT: To make it clearer what we are talking about: take the example of Bailey [a neighbor's black lab retriever] . . .

TONI: Yes, Bailey.

PARTICIPANT: With him it's kind of clear . . . playing with him, watching him run, feeling the sun, the connection, the communication with this dog—it's natural. But then I'm thinking, "Well, what if right at that time this dog dies?" You know?

TONI: Yes.

PARTICIPANT: So can there be . . . and this is not my experience, but I'm wondering . . . is there a presence so strong that it's clearly seen: here is the dead dog's body and, though the energy has changed, nothing has died.

TONI: Yes. It was somewhat like that at the time of Kyle's dying and death. And yet, for quite a while, the physical bodymind had its own momentum. Clarity without the pain of loss wasn't immediate. What came first was deeply felt attachment and wanting and grieving. It was the retreat two weeks later that made it possible to remember Kyle without the throbbing ache of attachment. But that requires moment-to-moment living with intense energy of presence that severs memories from their painful attachments. Presence bare of attachment. But in our normal way of living, the energy of remembered past experiences dominates—the energy of pleasure, wanting, missing, and painful grieving. It is what the Buddhists call the relative world of samsara. When energy is operating on that level, there is attachment with its inevitable fear of loss—the pain and suffering, wanting.

You know, just this morning as John was picking me up, he said, "Look, there's Bailey." The lovable tail-wagging, drooling black dog was standing high on the little brick wall, looking down and licking his chops in anticipation of the biscuit he usually gets when I greet him at the door. My pockets were empty, and I didn't want to go back into the house to get a treat for him. I said, "Bye, Bailey, I'll give you a cookie when I come back." He looked sad yet dignified, you know? It was different from what he expected, but he didn't bark—just stood there watching quietly and after a while just walked away. As we drove up the hill, Bailey was entirely gone from my mind. No sorrow, no regret.

This was nothing like the magnitude of death with Kyle's parting. When you have lived together for over fifty years, something happens between you that cannot and need not be denied or ignored. But it can be watched carefully and learned from. Buddhists say that the problem with relationship isn't the pleasure it gives but the *attachment* that grows out of it. In other words, everything is OK as long as I don't get attached. Again, I can't help saying, "Wait a minute! There *is* unavoidable attachment on the relative level that is our habitual living space." Not to argue it away ideologically, but to *watch* it.

And then there's the possibility of being in a field—no, *field* is not a good word. This is not a field, not a "state." Presence is not a "state." A "state" has boundaries in time and in space. But in that "non-state" of presence you can be so close to the painful wound that it no longer festers or hurts.

So we need to be careful—that is why it's good to always have the opportunity to ask questions, to clarify. This "inevitability of attachment" is on the relative level, not in any fundamental sense. Or if someone insists, "I'm not going to get attached; I'll prove it to you!" then often there is violence done to oneself. Repression. The "me" disciplining the "me," in a state of duality. But attachment returns through the back door. It never works, really, unless presence comes into play with its absence of willpower and resistance, but clarity of seeing instead.

Now, tell me just a little bit where you were coming from in raising this question, unless you don't want to touch something personal, . . .

PARTICIPANT: Well, you know, I wondered because there was something about this word *inevitability*. Because, you know, we change, things change, so how can we say it's inevitable that attachment has to happen? Do we know that?

TONI: Let me follow that. Again, why can't we say it's inevitable? What is the reason?

PARTICIPANT: OK. Yes, if it is clarified that attachment is inevitable in the relative world, then, yes, I agree with you. I guess I was thinking that you weren't considering that when this other—presence—comes, then there is the possibility of not getting attached. Because then there isn't this going into the love story, and the pain of that, because one sees it.

TONI: The seeing is the ending of that.

PARTICIPANT: Yes. [pause] And now I'm looking . . . there can also be the fear of getting involved because of the suffering that has come from that in the past.

TONI: Fear of getting involved because I may get attached again, and then suffering will come from that.

PARTICIPANT: Yes, yes. And thinking I don't want to suffer that way. So we bring that kind of attitude to living. It's fear.

TONI: Yes. Maybe it's fear, but it might also be simple intelligence.

PARTICIPANT: [*laughing*] Yes!

TONI: [*laughing*] Yes! What is it?

17

Two Responses to September 11

Response One

Out of this darkest of moods was born the question that kept propelling me from then on to find an answer beyond all doubt: What is the meaning of this totally senseless, fear-ridden life?

DEAR MATTHEW,

You are asking for a few paragraphs reflecting my thoughts on the events of 9/11 from the standpoint of awakening—how our belief in being a "separate individual" is the root cause of fear, anxiety, and the desire to "do something" about these events.

Rather than start from the "standpoint of awakening," let me go briefly into the events of my early youth that became the seeds for sustained questioning.

Even though we lived in a city (Leipzig), with industry surrounding it, we were never bombed until December 4, 1943. A large squadron of bombers had set out for Berlin, the capital, which had been bombed heavily almost every night. Because this night an unusually large number of planes were approaching, Leipzig sent its firefighting and antiaircraft equipment to Berlin to help out. However, instead of targeting Berlin, the squadron made a sharp turn toward Leipzig and dropped all of its cargo on the undefended city. The firebombs were placed in such a way that a strong windstorm developed, which kept the city burning for a week or longer. We didn't see much daylight during those days—the sky remained a darkish gray-yellow smoky veil. The streets were littered with debris, which included many partially burned papers—torn-up book pages—since Leipzig was the principal publishing center of Germany. Many people's houses that were not hit at the beginning of the attack caught on fire during the week of the storm. Our house was not damaged this time, and I do not remember the number of casualties—German media were not keen on publishing numbers. The surrounding industries remained mostly intact.

What is deeply imprinted in my memory is the depressed mood that set in right after the attack—the feeling of utter hopelessness and despair, not only because of the air raids that I knew would happen again and again, but also the constant fear that my mother, who was Jewish, could be deported to a concentration camp at any time, and the tormenting doubt whether there would ever be an end to the horrendous carnage of war.

Out of this darkest of moods was born the question that kept propelling me from then on to find an answer beyond all doubt: *What is the meaning of this totally senseless, fear-ridden life?*

My faith in God had shattered. I had seen my father, who had been a glowing model of brightness and equanimity for me all these years, sitting wrapped in a big gray coat in the dusty basement air-raid shelter of our house, his hat pulled deeply over his forehead, absorbed in faceless fear. No feeling of security remained, nothing left to trust. Only the question about the meaning of life stayed alive during the following years, and I searched countless books and engaged many people whom I respected for their knowledge and wisdom in verbal or tacit dialogue—to no deep satisfaction.

Eventually, after much study in the fields of psychology,

sociology, anthropology, philosophy, and mythology, I found meditation practice, which would put an end to all questions and doubts about life's ultimate meaning.

It is as clear as sunshine in a bright blue sky that there is no extra meaning to life—that life, just the way it is, changing from moment to moment in unexpected ways, does not point to any meaning beyond itself. Every moment is the result of the infinite past and is at the same time new, fresh, and free.

Quietly listening, at this moment of simple openness, there is no entity here who is fearing, wanting, or suffering—there *is* wanting and fearing and suffering the instant our thinking resists and fights what is here right now, and longs for what is not. Living each moment fully is totally different from dwelling in stories about it.

Right action does not flow out of reaction of any kind—be it fear, anger, revenge, thirst for justice, or yearning for the solace of belonging. Symbols such as crosses, swastikas, and colorful flags do not bring insight. They may provide inspirational energies and limited feelings of togetherness, but they cannot reveal this moment of wondrous presence, full of love, without any lack.

Response Two

Can we come back time and time again, with infinite patience, to what is actually taking place *right now*, this very moment?

Someone asked for a few words of advice for dealing with the torrent of feelings, emotions, and confusions that are coming up in the wake of the horrendous explosions inside and out that shook us all to the roots.

If possible, can we find a quiet moment in a quiet space in the midst of all the noise, agitation, and confusion; a quiet spot in the eye of sadness and grief, pain, anger, and rage; the urge for revenge; and the longing for security to end all suffering? Can we listen silently to the contractions of fear, anger, and the throbbing of longing for safety?

Can we listen ever more silently to the constant crowding of agitated reactions to what we are seeing happening on television or live in front of our eyes, thinking frantically about what could have happened, should have happened, or ought to happen in response to it all? Can moments of calm presence reveal the turmoil of thinking and emoting, staying with it all without being completely taken over by it?

Can we come back time and time again, with infinite patience, to what is actually taking place *right now*, this very moment—the sadness and grief paining heart and mind, fear knotting the stomach and guts, anger making the heart pound faster, driving the blood to the head, and also hear the sound of rain, motor noises around us, the brightness and darkness of the room, the sky, the smell in the air—not just the reactions to all of this, but simply perceiving sounds and sights and the feel of what is actually taking place?

Listening quietly to the cacophony of the inner and outer world, can we come upon a hidden silence that enfolds all the noise and confusion, the sky and smoke and buildings crumbled to the ground, the people in dust-covered coats searching the rubble for signs of life while balancing precariously on fallen rafters and bent steel beams?

This stillness has room for everything happening on this earth—the good and the evil, the wounding, the helping and the healing, the dying and living, the hating, the killing, and the inexhaustible love that transcends it all in a way too marvelous to comprehend.

18

Feeling Separate, Living Together

This is the beauty of silent meditative questioning and watching: the growing transparency of thoughts and images and their power to keep this body enmeshed in emotional drama, tragedy, and comedy.

HOW WARM THE MORNING after a freezing night! Earlier, transparent sheets of cloud were streaking across the blue sky. Now thicker ones are darkening the sunlight. The rumbling of an airplane . . .

Is it here? Is it an effort to hear the sound of the plane? Or is it simply here? Without needing to strain?

Breathing quietly. Is it here?

Breathing without the word. Without knowing about it. Just feeling it, in and out, in and out, touching this amazing movement without anyone doing it. Not thinking how breathing should be, such as "deep" or "yogic" or "natural." *What is it* as it is taking place right now? Can we listen quietly?

What are wind, quivering leaves, creaking branches, beating heart, without the words? We need words to talk to each other, but listening can be wordless. And if words pop up, as they do habitually, can we see them as just words? Do we realize that words, like "leaves quivering in the breeze," are not what is being described?

What are words *pointing to*? To find out, we need to stop all doing and listen quietly, effortlessly, without anticipating. Are words mingled in with the listening? Let them intermingle. Words are not what they are describing. What is the *real* thing?

Words are learned utterances evoked by memories, remembered feelings and stories in the mind, associated events, emotions such as delight, anger, or fear. But "openness" and "presence" are not just words or concepts. Presence is the whole world just as it is from moment to moment. Rumbling motors, chirping cicadas, breathing bodies, swirling leaves—can they happen freely without needing to be grasped or rejected? Without needing to be known?

Yesterday we talked about fear being generated by feelings of separation and isolation, an imagined sense of disconnect between me and the world, me and you, me and "God." The idea of separation produces anxiety. The haunting thought and feeling of being lonely, abandoned, unloved, secretes fear. People mention this a lot and we discuss it in meetings, trying to understand closely what is actually happening within us when we say that we're afraid. Can each one of us track down, like a detective, what we actually refer to when we say, "I'm feeling isolated and lonely, and it makes me feel anxious?" What is going on *physically*, not just conceptually?

This brain-body quickly shifts away from physically experiencing momentary pain or pleasure to living in words, describing in vivid story lines what has happened to us. The entire organism reacts dramatically to these stories long after the actual event is over, still responding emotionally with stress, pleasure, joy, pain, tears, laughter. It is really amazing how a story that composed itself ex post facto about an incident evokes the same feelings as the actual experience did. A remembered story is capable of eliciting remembered feelings years and even lifetimes after the actual experiences have passed away.

So, can we track down what we mean when we say we feel separate? What *is* this feeling of separation? What *is* this isolation? How does it manifest? Stop for a moment and quietly watch it! Watch how the body reacts with all kinds of sensations and tensions to remembered words and images. Observe it with interest and wonder, without the need to do anything about it! Quiet watching has its own silent wisdom and action.

Yesterday as I drove up the driveway, several deer stood scattered across the road, some grown ones and two young dappled fawns staring motionlessly at the approaching car. I drove very slowly, then stopped close to them. We looked at each other for a silent while, and then I drove on slowly. The grown deer walked carefully into the woods without rush, without leaving the fawns out of sight. Without spoken language they communicated clearly with one another. A mother deer, hiding in the tree brush, snorted furiously to attract the fawns' attention, intermittently stomping her front hoof onto the ground. She seemed to be prodding the newly born ones to join her in the thicket. Eventually, the curious, big-eyed fawns obliged, disappearing behind the trees.

Do deer brains produce concepts such as "separation"? Do they evoke ideas of "being isolated," "abandoned," "unloved"? Very unlikely! They hover and move about in groups most of the time, but this is most probably for comfort and survival. It is highly improbable that story lines arise in their brains: "We're lonely, we're abandoned, we're unloved." I don't think they ever feel sorry for themselves! They do learn quickly to see and understand danger, and instinctively respond appropriately without unnecessary sentiments.

Do we begin to realize how our feelings are tightly interconnected with remembered thoughts and images? Can we witness time and again, during sitting and daily living, how fearful feelings arise from remembered thought and story, how the panorama of physical sensations and emotions is intimately tied up with the flow of remembered incidents in the form of words and pictures?

Once the brain gets verbally involved with physical pains, aches, and tensions, it also creates the assumption that feelings and sensations must be about something real. Since the paining or pleasuring body is very real, it seems to follow that it must also be real what the pain or pleasure is all about. The story assumes the power of "virtual reality."

We hear, imagine, and watch so many stories! Our life is becoming more and more inundated with TV shows, movies, videos, magazines, and newspaper articles that seem to show and tell us what life is like. And then the inevitable comparisons arise: "My life isn't like that," or "I wish it were," or "It is exactly like that." The moment we notice painful or sad feelings arising from thoughts like "I'm unloved; I feel separate and isolated," can we immediately stop, look, and listen instead of going on weaving fancy narratives about ourselves? Can we stop and ask, "Where is this feeling coming from?" Right now. Asking right this moment. Becoming more transparent to thoughts and images that *evoke* these feelings and then deepen, embellish, and propagate them. We often feel impelled to share our stories with others to get reinforcement for them. We seek sympathetic audiences that strengthen our sad or happy life stories.

Becoming aware, let us taste directly how stories run our lives and seem so real as they trigger concrete manifestations in the body: increasing heartbeat, tensing muscles, churning stomach and intestines, blood rushing into the head causing a throbbing. Very often people insist that sensations and emotions just happen for no known reason. No thought was detected that could have triggered sensations of fear or anger. Then, it is argued, how can anyone assert that feelings and sensations are linked directly with thoughts and images?

This is the beauty of silent meditative questioning and watching: the growing transparency of thoughts and images and their power to keep this body enmeshed in emotional drama, tragedy, and comedy.

You may say, "Wait a minute, wait a minute. There isn't just the *thought* that I'm not loved—there truly is no one in my life who loves me. It's a *fact* that I have no friends. It's a fact that people don't like me."

Be careful not to get stuck in conclusions. You may be mistaken, or what *was* may not *be* so any longer. Test it out anew. Is it really true that you are not liked, without friends? How do you really know? And if it still seems to be that way, *why* do you think that?

Let us look, for a moment, at how we relate to one another. We've touched upon this many times before. We are usually so voluminously involved in our personal problems that they seem to be taking up our entire living space. We are brimful with self-concern: "What is going to happen to me in the future? Will my needs be met? My wishes and hopes? Will my way prevail? My rights? My convictions? No one has as heavy a past history as I do—that's my unique fate."

Constant self-interest and self-indulgence does not attract friends. One feels compelled to defend and explain oneself in order to appear in the right light. Most of the time other people are not really interested in one's story, particularly not if they sense the surreptitious demand to commiserate with it. We don't like to feel imposed upon. It can repel others.

On the other hand, it is a heartwarming experience to be with someone who is selflessly present, listening without wanting anything. That spontaneously evokes love and affection, doesn't it? Selflessness presents itself in a relaxed, natural way of being, in plenty of breathing space that invites genuine connection, communion. People gravitate naturally toward a person who allows space for closeness and natural expression. Have you noticed that love genuinely flows toward such a person?

Out of the space of no-self arises the energy and vision to do something together—not in order to gain admiration and gratitude but because it is the most natural thing in the world to be connected, at-one, and help each other if needed. In that there is no self-conscious "doing good for others."

I hope this didn't sound like advocating the cultivation of self-lessness. Love cannot be "cultivated"—it is not a moral principle to be learned in lessons. It wells up and unfolds naturally when the conditions are ripe.

With space comes lightness, affection, *Zuneigung.* The German word *Zuneigung* literally means "affectionately leaning toward another." With natural affection for others, feelings of isolation or separation do not exist. There is freedom from thoughts about how worthy or unworthy I am, how unloved, how isolated. Words that we have repeated to ourselves over and over in story lines do not tell the truth, and that fact is suddenly and deeply understood.

19

Togetherness

Discover that in the simple question "Does it have to go on in this way?" a break appears in the seemingly endless chain of mind habits. Awareness can actually take the place of thinking!

THIS WHOLE BODYMIND is overflowing with joy and gratitude for being here with you. Every retreat is an unexpected gift! One doesn't know ahead of time whether it will all come to pass, but here we are as one whole—everything taking care of itself.

With the overflowing sense of love and well-being goes a genuine urge to share it with others. To share it with everyone interested in looking and listening, with people who at this moment may feel sad, isolated, and unloved. All of us are these people at one time or other—feeling painfully cut off from each other yet longing for togetherness, closeness, spontaneity, and real being.

Feeling cut off from others is created by the mind, a thought system that has unlimited capacity to feel things that are not really true but only imagined, such as the image of being an abandoned, lonesome person, not seen or liked by others, not good enough for them and therefore rejected. If this retreat can serve us to become directly aware of such painful ideas and images coalescing into stories, to see them as just that, and to witness their emotional power within, then there will also be the energy to question if things really *have* to be this way. When there is free-dom to question ourselves honestly, it will have been worthwhile to spend time here together in solitude and silence.

The first meditative step is *detecting* our constant wishful thinking for a better life, a clearer state of mind, and the hope of attaining it or the fear of not getting it. Can we just stop for a mo-ment in silence and question whether wishing and fearing have to keep going? Do they? Right now we may not know. Can we earnestly question whether *anything* spun out by the thinking mind has to keep on going? Does the habit of fantasizing a better state have to continue as it is clearly observed? Maybe it does, maybe not. Let's find out! Does it need to be identified with— "these are *my* wishes"—rationalized, or excused in any way? Does thinking need to hang on to the consolation that this is the way we have been conditioned and that therefore nothing can change? Or can we unexpectedly come upon the amazing freedom to question everything about ourselves? Discover that in the sim-ple question "Does it have to go on in this way?" a break appears in the seemingly endless chain of mind habits. Awareness can actually take the place of thinking!

Normally fantasies are spinning out one after another, usually about being someplace else or being different from what we are right now. What about a moment of stopping and checking whether this is going on right now? Simply waking up this mo-ment to what is taking place right now, opening up to . . . noth-ing special. Just wind blowing, windows rattling, birds calling, breath flowing in and out, bright sunshine filtering through the shades making patterns on the floor. When that happens, it is clear that no wishing has brought it about! Being here now in unadorned simplicity is our true state—whole and inseparable from anything else.

Right now are we about to get caught up in desiring this won-derful-sounding "state of wholeness," or are we aware of what is going on—the dreaming, fearing, wishing, and holding on to the spinning around inside the head? In simple awareness of the constant "me"-drama, there is now a touch of presence. Maybe even a sense of well-being that accompanies open awareness.

There are several kinds of well-being. One suddenly presents itself out of nowhere, filling this bodymind and lighting up everything everywhere. The other kind arises out of dreaming about wonderful states. This has great emotional power over the entire body but fizzles out when the dream ends. It may be healthier to entertain pleasant thoughts than give way to doomsday feelings—that painful negativity we so often carry around with us like an infectious virus.

But just learning to switch thoughts from negative to positive is not enough, helpful though it may be for the time being. A direct insight is needed into the moment-to-moment inner drama taking place in thought and image. It's not necessary to name it. It's OK when a description about "you" and "me" comes up in words. We communicate in that way. But the momentary and ever-changing internal show need not be known by a "knower," who always creates distance and time. Insight is immediate without subject or object. What is seen is let go again into emptiness.

I saw a neat little Brit-com on TV the other evening. A stretcher with a woman lying on it was rolled out of an emergency room in a hospital. Right next to it walked a tall, good-looking white man, and behind it a diminutive dark-haired woman, who looked Indian. The husband of the patient, visibly anxious to find out about the state of the woman, asks the tall man, "Doctor, please tell me what are her chances?" And the diminutive dark-skinned woman replies, "I'm the doctor; he's the nurse."

It's a humorous example of how we live and relate. It's not our fault. We are programmed by mountains of past experiences, including our genes. Experiences and their feelings and emotions as well as stories we have been told since time immemorial are registered and stored in the brain. These brain patterns automatically steer thoughts and actions. They are seldom questioned for any kind of accuracy—we are taking the accuracy of images about ourselves and others almost totally for granted.

Already my family and all their ancestors, their teachers, friends, and neighbors, as well as what I think is my own personal intuition have told me, or subtly intimated, that people who look different from my kind are inferior and not to be fully trusted. In these archetypal programs questioning does not exist. I'm not saying that our programmed bodymind prevents all questioning from happening. Questioning happens in spite of it all! We may suddenly begin to see and think for ourselves. How this happens is a mystery to me. After the fact, we can describe poetically that the clouds suddenly parted and revealed the ever-present sun sparkling brightly. When that happens, you and I do not see different worlds—it's just one seamless whole seeing that defies description or explanation.

I'm an avid news watcher, passionately following political developments on TV and in print. When something special is going on, such as an election or a war, the public TV channel gathers together focus groups in different cities to find out different people's opinions. At times a focus group takes place in a school or college and the young people become the communicators. The intelligence and clear thinking of some of these students is so refreshing compared to the comments of older folks, who seem to be more firmly set in their opinions. The younger ones still seem to have some freedom from stagnation and are open to questioning illogical or incoherent statements by the politicians. This seems to be an aspect of our native intelligence that sooner or later gets smothered by education and indoctrination. I don't know. But even for adults it remains possible to question cherished assumptions, dangerous though it may seem. The imagined danger is ostracism from the group.

This fear of being shunned or ostracized is deeply embedded in most living beings. We all seek security through acceptance by the group. We don't want to be punished for questioning or dissenting. Ostracism was the harshest of ancient punishments. We long to remain part of the community that gives us the safety of identity and energy.

But still, for no known reason, human beings like you and me do have the ability to question and think intelligently. We may just be groping around for a while, making all kinds of mistakes. But there is this irrepressible urge in most living beings for light and clarity. Many great religious leaders have pronounced throughout the ages that human beings carry within themselves the yearning and energy to break out of darkness—to find clarity out of delusion. That takes constant questioning, because the delusions of ideas and convictions in and around us are so very powerful.

So here we are together supporting each other in an amazing way, even though we don't really know each other or need to talk to each other. The light we are groping for is here. It helps us in seeing what constitutes blindness, darkness. The need for the pseudo security of being "me." Not to condemn that movement but to see it, to feel it as it happens and understand it with kindness, and a bit of space left for wondering whether it is really safe to follow our ingrained ideas about "me" and the so-called "others"!

It's a monumental thing to even think of questioning that, because we don't have much social support for such an undertaking. And yet throughout the ages there has been this light flashing brightly, here or there—the light of clarity, of truth and love—and the urge to share it with others. Not to convert or to conquer or annihilate with word and sword. Light shines out of love and wisdom, which are not values in any normal sense. Normal values are relative. This is not. Love is not relative. It is absolute—that is, it depends on nothing.

20

Honesty

Even though this bodymind is "wired" with a thousand painful and pleasant memories of past hurts and pleasures, is it possible to live fully this present moment and allow the power of awareness to short-circuit old pathways of memory? Let presence be the circuit breaker! Let awareness, with its love and wisdom, clear up our clogged channels.

WHAT ABOUT HONESTY? I recall somebody saying, "I wish we would at least be honest with each other, telling each other honestly how we feel about each other rather than being hypocritically nice or saying nothing at all. Or, what is even worse, talk to others about it." Such statements are very compelling, and the word *honesty* has a tremendous moral weight to it. We believe that to be dishonest is a terrible fault.

In school in Germany we had to recite a verse that began, "Above all else, my child, be faithful, honest, and true. Never let a lie escape your lips, because since ancient times the highest virtue among the German people was to be faithful and honest."

The poem inculcates the child with a moral attitude toward honesty and warns severely about telling lies. But is something overlooked in this "being honest" and ignored in "telling lies"?

Can you honestly be honest when you know you will get punished for what you say? If in the past you have gotten blamed or misunderstood for telling honestly how you felt about a person, will you now feel free to speak openly to him or her? Can you trust that you will be truly heard and understood? Or will you automatically expect people to turn against you again for what you say? Will people whom you told honestly about your feelings pass it on to others, who may turn against you? This mind is such a tight preserver of memories (whether they are accurate or not), and it can react instantly from these memories.

The brain collects pictures about one's imagined self and others. So if I tell you honestly how I feel about you at this moment, this information (correct or incorrect) can remain lodged in your mind for a very long time, creating and maintaining a palpable dis-ease between us. It will prevent us from relating in an open, unencumbered way. It's easy to say, "I want you to be honest with me—tell me how you truly feel about me." Will it actually happen that way? It can happen if we are both sure to remain open to questioning, listening and looking together without trying to keep our beloved images intact. It can happen if neither of us closes up or switches to defense or attack when we hear unpleasant things about ourselves. I remember one time thinking I had this kind of trusting relationship with a friend, so I spoke honestly about how I felt about something he had said. But he did get offended and resentful after all, and our relationship was marred. Memory stored the whole incident and warned, "Be careful next time because you can't trust he will not get offended again. And it is difficult to live with people who harbor insults."

Are we willing (as we may be here in retreat) to remain open to feeling hurt, and to question deeply why it happens, why we feel rejected, and whether it *has* to happen this way time and again? Questioning it thoroughly, unconditionally, and not assuming it's inevitable? Are we willing to allow clear thinking (wisdom) to operate when images are getting hurt? To feel the rejection? Can we see and understand how images are wired into this sensitive brain and body? See and understand how living a life of images is a very dangerous and painful way of living that need not continue the moment clear awareness dawns.

Somebody said, "I used to be so reactive to my mother. She pushed all my buttons. And then something amazing happened. She can say something to me now and I am able to listen quietly. It doesn't push the reactive buttons any longer." Can this happen with other relationships too? With someone who has hurt us many times before? Even though this bodymind is "wired" with a thousand painful and pleasant memories of past hurts and pleasures, is it possible to live fully this present moment and allow the power of awareness to short-circuit old pathways of memory? Let presence be the circuit breaker! Let awareness, with its love and wisdom, clear up our clogged channels. *Short-circuiting* is a good word because this is how it feels. The "offensive" remark doesn't overpower the system and thus can't trigger a defensive reaction. The spark doesn't fly! And even if it has sparked, it can be seen. Seeing turns it off, dissolves it.

No new scars are needed. Let old scars dissolve as they come into view. Particularly in a quiet retreat, but also in our daily living. Unfortunately we normally don't take the time to sit quietly with upset and let it unfold. Let's take the time to look beyond offense and defenses that come up routinely. After all, what is this whole business of "me" and "you" other than thought and image fluff—powerful bodily sensations and feelings that are intertwined with old memories?

Listen to the leaves rustling in the breeze right now! That's not memory, is it? You may have a mental picture of a tree gently swaying in the breeze. But the immediacy of sound and sight is not memory. Presence can never be memory. It has nothing to do with time. It's just what's here and here and here.

Now. Crickets chirping.

21

Despair

When there is complete presence (not meaning that "you" or "I" am present but that there is simply presence), then questions like "Is this enough? Is there something else? Is this all?" become meaningless. Questions like these arise out of our habitual state of discontent with what is.

THE FIRST QUESTION in the group last night spread around quickly, filling up the entire time. "What is despair?"

We don't experience just one kind of despair. There's despair about the world situation, politics, the increasing complications of warfare from the smallest scale to the largest with unimaginable side effects, and then there is the despair arising out of feelings of helplessness, hopelessness, and the frustrating incapacity to do anything worthwhile about it. As people were bringing up their personal despair, it became clear that there is always a thread of ideas, of thinking, of "shoulds" and "ought nots" that result in avalanching despair.

One person remarked, "I feel I ought to achieve something significant in my life, something I haven't accomplished yet." Some people felt the pressure of time in the urgency to leave something of value behind, something that would survive their earthly existence. In Zen training centers, especially during retreats, we were forcefully reminded that "time waits for no one!"

"If you're not getting enlightened in this retreat, when will you?" was frequently shouted by roshi and monitors during sittings. Before ending the formal daily schedule each evening, the head monk would passionately exclaim to the ear-shattering pounding of a wooden block:

Strive through the night with all your breath
That you may wake past day, past death!

The rising crescendo of voice and wooden block aroused a jolting shuddering throughout the hall. In addition, we were repeatedly reminded of past masters' admonishments to their disciples to stop wasting time and work ever harder. (This in spite of the fact that the Buddha, at the time of his enlightenment, was said to have exclaimed, "I truly attained nothing from supreme unsurpassed enlightenment!")

Nothing to achieve, nothing to attain!

A powerful conviction permeated the practice that enormous amounts of effort had to be expended before one would realize the truth of "nothing to attain."

Just a couple of days before my husband, Kyle, died, he uttered in despair while lifting his arms up and down—the only movement still possible for his weakened body, "Oh my, oh my, I have achieved nothing in my life, nothing!" I remember laying my head on his chest and gently whispering into his ear, "You're here, Kyle. You're here!" With that the lamenting fell silent.

Did those words hit the painful spot of doubt, wiping it out in gentle meeting? You're here, Kyle! We're here!

Isn't that entirely sufficient?

Doubting thoughts may quickly reply, "No, it isn't enough! What does it mean anyway, this 'being here'?" The moment such thoughts arise—"No, it's not enough"—and ask for further explanations, one is no longer here! When there is complete presence (not meaning that "you" or "I" am present but that there is simply presence), then questions like "Is this enough? Is there something else? Is this all?" become meaningless. Questions like these arise out of our habitual state of discontent with what is.

When I was a child, my father gave me a small camera. In order to focus it properly, you had to look through the viewfinder and see two little transparent rectangles superimposed upon the scenery. By turning the viewfinder back and forth, these two windows moved either farther apart or closer together until just a single window remained. With that the entire picture came into sharp focus. This process impressed itself deeply on my mind: the possibility of a picture being in complete focus, neither speeding ahead nor lagging behind, neither too far to the right nor off to the left.

Coming into full focus doesn't happen through thinking; words won't bring it about. Being in proper focus happens by being right here, right now—not caught in the viewfinder of the "me" moving back and forth. When the image of "me" fades out in the vast energy field of simply being here, just hearing the sounds of voice and wind, breathing, sneezing, and coughing—when there is just this and none of the habitual evaluations and comparisons, the whole "me"-circuit quietly unplugs. There is no longer any meaningful "more" or "not enough." Those concepts become amazingly irrelevant. They don't even arise. Every instant of presence—that is, here-ness and now-ness—is totally sufficient unto itself!

No one can give this to you because it is already present! All that's needed is to awaken from the clouds of thought-created "me"-existence. In thought-created existence with "me" at the center, there is either happiness or despair, and the constant struggle to retain the one or get rid of the other. Thoughts like "The world is going from bad to worse" or "I'm not creating anything worthwhile to help out" can only flourish in the shadow of thought-created existence.

So mentioning our despair about water and air pollution, the cutting down of trees resulting in deforestation, and their dire consequences . . . thinking all these things makes our hearts ache with despair, and something wants to cry out, "Stop! Hold it! Go no farther! Just look for an instant at what is happening right now with all this incessant thinking and imagining!" Can there be a fresh moment of just *being*?

A few years ago I watched a news segment with Dan Rather reporting from Somalia. He had gone far out into the desert with a few soldiers where no visible habitation existed except for a small number of tents where some physicians from Doctors Without Borders were doing their work. He wanted to broadcast "in the raw" the amazing operations they were performing. Just as Rather and his crew had arrived, a little baby was brought in whose skull had been severely punctured by bullets. The doctor appeared calm, doing what she could to bandage the tiny bleeding head. At one point she had to turn away in order to reach for an instrument on a table, and she asked Dan Rather to steady the baby for a moment to keep it from rolling off. Dan held the baby and, with incredible tenderness and just a couple of fingers, massaged a tiny foot. Two fingers were almost too big! He was visibly shaken by the whole thing and asked the doctor whether this baby would live. She didn't know. He repeated his question and her answer was, "Maybe another four weeks; it's too hard to tell."

Here was this courageous woman in the middle of nowhere, carefully patching up a tiny infant's head, not at all certain that it would even outlive the month! She was truly not working for results but simply doing the work of this moment, without agonizing about yesterday or tomorrow. And so was Dan Rather: in tenderly massaging the baby's toes, the famous anchor had totally disappeared.

A lot of people have learned, and can learn at any time, that the despair gripping this organism with all its electrochemical currents can actually abate when something real is undertaken— when something concrete takes the place of just thinking about it. Maybe just going for a walk, or merely stepping outside the house to take in a breath of fresh air. These simple actions do not get entangled in the thought process of "Is there is any hope left for helping humankind?"

Learning to clearly discern when we are stuck in a futile circuit of ideas and their verbalization is of vital importance, because the very way that we formulate the situation (of the world or of my-self) has a tremendous impact on this bodymind. Not just the raw situation as it is perceived but how we put it to ourselves in lan-guage—that is the extra whammy. So often we continue living in the story while the incident has long since passed. The story can keep on going, keeping the bodymind irritated and out of balance. At any moment of waking up to *now* from story-life, can we ask, "What is going on right now? Am I wrapped up in a story?" and "Does it have to continue this way?" We may notice to our amaze-ment that we feel a strong attachment to this story! We do not want to let go of it, even if it's a miserable and painful story! We cling to our descriptions as though they were the real things!

How readily can we step out of the story back into the real mo-ment of aliveness? Language may be misleading here. There is no "me" doing it. It's just a palpable exchange of circuitry, and there-fore a change affecting the entire body. From dreaming, fantasiz-ing, thinking, recollecting, anticipating to . . . here. Here! Now! Breathing in and out. Yawning. Heart beating. Maybe stomach aching. Faint sounds of traffic, a fan humming. No "inside" or "outside." People moving about. Laughter. Distant talking . . .

Here open listening is not used as a technique for distraction. Switching from dreaming to wakefulness is not a technique! Being here is our true nature. Our true being is *here*.

The human brain (together with the entire organism) has a wondrous capacity to live in alternating scenarios, and providing the body with a lively accompaniment which makes each plot ap-pear so utterly real—we feel the fear, experience the anger, sense the heart pounding, perceive the blood rising into the head, and suffer all the tensions in the musculature. This is not theoretical but palpably concrete. But the screenplay that is being accompanied is not concrete. It is a fabrication of thought, memory, and idea. We often say, "The very idea of all this makes me mad," or "I'm happy beyond words!"

Many comments were made in our discussion about despair. There is much truth in them, and a lot that is false. For instance, it's true that despair is an individual affair, that each one of us may feel it differently. What makes me feel despair may make you quite happy. We can watch that in the TV broadcasts of wars, where one side rejoices while the enemy weeps. This holds true for both sides, each applauding while the others suffer despair.

It's sad how much we are blinded by our sheer ignorance about what *we* are and what the *others* are not. If miraculously, this very moment, the veils of self-deception could drop from our soldiers' eyes—if our brains could clear themselves of false images about "self" and "others"—not another shot to kill would be fired from any of the soldiers' guns. This has actually recently happened to some officers and troops in Israel—some of these warriors were recorded as saying, "What in the hell are we doing killing our brethren?"

I don't believe human beings are inherently evil. I cannot believe that for one instant. Just because horrendous deeds are committed doesn't mean that the perpetrators are inherently and incorrigibly evil. If we were to search a bit into the personal life histories of people and their families after generations of suffering unspeakable horrors, the whole human drama could, maybe, explain itself simply and clearly: This leads to that. Things would have, or else wouldn't have, happened this or that way, given all the circumstances. Thich Nhat Hahn once expressed in a poem that if he had been born in another country to different parents, he, too, could have become a rapist. . . .

A simple man, a steel worker, came to Springwater Center once. He had been a soldier in Vietnam, and told me how he had been sent on a mission that would entail certain death, and how he felt unspeakably frightened, hopeless, and then . . . I think his words were something like: "Then suddenly, flying the helicopter on its mission, all there was left was being bathed in love with not the slightest fear of death, everything being all right the way it was." And then, he recalled, "We couldn't even find our target and the mission was called off—we turned around toward where we had started from!" He tried to tell some of his platoon buddies what had happened to him on the flight, but they just thought he had flipped. Flipped a circuit in his brain. And maybe he had. We could all use such flips.

I'm mentioning this story to illustrate that awakening can happen at any time, to anyone, particularly when the despair is total. No way out. Certain death. Nothing left to hold on to, to identify with. It's clear that for that soldier there was nothing left to cling to. So where is the despair? Or the hope? Aren't these all factors in what we call the relative life, the life of conditioning, in contrast to what Easterners call the Absolute, that which holds on to nothing and depends on nothing? In that there is no despair and no hope—no me. The troublemaker is absent. So, can there be at least a slight taste now and then of what has been called the Unconditioned?

There are some beautiful words from the Buddha: "Monks, there is an unborn, unbecome, unmade, unconditioned. Monks, if there were not an unborn, unbecome, unmade, unconditioned, then we could not here know any escape from the born, become, made, conditioned. . . ."*

And that escape, that way out is not, as we may have been led to believe, a long, arduous path into the future. Our conditioned earthly life is indeed a long and arduous path—that is an undeniable fact. At times interspersed with wonderful "vacations"! But

---

* *Udana in Khuddaka-nikaya*, in *The Buddhist Experience: Sources and Interpretations*, trans. Stephan Beyer (Encino, Calif.: Dickenson, 1974), pp. 199–200.

the true way out is right here, now. It cannot be attained, or approached, or hoped for in the distant future or in another lifetime because it is here. Right here, this very instant!

Can there be a waking up from our beclouded life of dreams? No strings can be attached to what is totally Unconditioned—it is without any recognizable form. It cannot be seen with our eyes, as it is that which makes that very seeing possible. It has been called the Light behind the Eyes that See.

22

Judgment: Is There Good and Bad?

Investigate not just the *incident* we're so upset over but also *our own upset*. Is it genuine? Genuine horror at what happened? Genuine compassion? Or is the you-versus-me syndrome alive and active to the extent that I cannot look at myself and everything is projected onto the other?

WE FREQUENTLY SAY to ourselves and to each other, "Don't judge!" And we can easily verify that the moment we fall into judging, it interrupts the simplicity of being present, of letting whatever arises in the mind come and go again.

This "going again" happens when no "me" is invested in the judgment—no attachment created to *my* particular ways—no insistence upon being right. Wherever there is judgment there is also a judge. Incessantly wanting to be something, we become a judge who passes judgment over oneself and others.

When we discussed this yesterday, someone brought up the fundamental question of whether there is really any good and bad, right and wrong. "After all," one person said, "one of the most wonderful Buddhist sutras says, 'The great way is not difficult for those who have no preferences.'"*

In other words, no thoughts of good or bad. Later on it says, "Make the smallest distinction, however, and heaven and earth are set infinitely apart."

Do you wonder what is meant by that? What is good and bad? Does that imply the presence of a judge immediately setting herself apart above others, remaining opaque to herself but shining the spotlight of judgment on others? When our wondering and examining mind includes the one who is passing judgments, only then does it become a wholesome inquiry and not just finding fault with others.

To say that there are no good and bad points to a meditative state of mind that is in no way divisive, be it mentally, spiritually, or physically. It is a state of just seeing clearly what is going on and yet realizing that certain rules and precepts are important for the healthy functioning of society. In Buddhism keeping the precepts (virtues) is considered inseparable from enlightenment. So it is not that Buddhism teaches there is no right and wrong, no morality. According to most Buddhist teachings, you can't consider yourself on the right path of enlightenment if you do not live a virtuous life. In light of that, you can't say that whatever a teacher does, such as having sex with the wife or husband of a student, is beyond reproach.

Only when there is illuminating wholeness—that is, no division into "you" and "me"—do virtue and compassion arise spontaneously.

I've often mentioned as an example something that happened to me early in this work of meditative inquiry. My habit had been

---

* *hsin hsin ming,* trans. Richard B. Clarke (Buffalo, N. Y.: White Pines Press, 1973).

to thoughtlessly swat mosquitoes that landed on my body, or to step on crawling insects if they were "in the way." We did this as little kids—crunching ants or other bugs with our shoes, not thinking anything about it. Then one day, after I had started practicing Zen, I saw a mosquito crawling on the piano in the playroom, and then another one alighted on my arm. Without any conscious intention to be good, I found myself watching the mosquito landing on the arm, stinging through the skin, and sucking up blood, its belly growing red and fat, almost too heavy for take-off. Watching all this happened totally without thinking about any precepts or intention to be compassionate; it arose out of sheer presence, observing with genuine interest, almost affection, without a judgmental thought affecting the mind.

From this and other examples I can say with deep conviction that when there is presence, with its clarity of observation, there is also genuine affection for other creatures and naturally refraining from hurting them. Hurting happens when there is inattention, self-centeredness, thinking of my rights or my way, being clever in riding roughshod over someone else. That all comes from inattention and self-absorption. They're almost the same things. But when attention is there without self-absorption, we see everything differently. We see one another's vulnerabilities clearly and also anticipate that what I am about to say to you could hurt you, and I don't have the slightest intention to hurt you.

When anger arises, I see quite clearly that it can feel good to give you a piece of my mind. But I also realize that I am very likely going to be misunderstood in hurting you, and it may evoke some form of retaliation. That's how we function. Even holy scriptures say "an eye for an eye, a tooth for a tooth." Imagine that—written down in a holy scripture! Somebody takes your eye or tooth, so you in turn can take his eye or tooth. What a strange ethic this is! We may think that we don't have such strange ethics, but many of us don't blink at having an assassin strapped into an electric chair to be electrocuted. Since he has killed someone, we kill him in return. In one case we think killing is wrong; in the other case we think it is right! How strange it is, both right and wrong!

Think about all of that and discuss it together, not just arguing one position against the other, fighting to be the winner of the debate. We are winners if we begin to illuminate positions and illuminate our identifications with our positions—identifications with "my" people, "my" ethnic group, "my" family, "my" whatever group. Do let all that come into awareness—seeing the tremendous power of division! "My people" versus those "others," in whom different feelings and emotions have been programmed. It is an amazing discovery: our instant desire for retaliation, wishing that the same thing or even worse happen to people on the opposite side. Can we actually see that in ourselves? Not just the craving for punishment of the guilty party, but the totally nonsensical ways in which we deal with each other.

Have you seen the movie *Shoah*? It's a nine-hour-long motion picture about the Holocaust. I was deeply impressed by this film, which was made at the actual locations where those events happened, mostly in Poland: the extermination areas of Auschwitz, remnants of the brick gas ovens, and train tracks leading directly into those places of horror.

A lot of the people shown were present-day folk who had had some part in the events and reminisced about them. Most of what you saw of the past was the villages—little houses and churches with their gardens and landscapes now overgrown with trees, meadows, and weeds.

Even though at that time I was a child (of a Jewish mother), I knew next to nothing about most of the story because my parents tried strenuously to keep us ignorant of all the horrible goings-on in the concentration camps. Yet children have very astute insight into the minds of their parents. For instance, we weren't allowed in the room while our parents listened to the BBC, but we had a notion what was being whispered about and that these were horribly bizarre events, to say the least. We could read in the adult faces the frightening things they had just heard. Later on, when we could talk about it, nobody in our family really knew most of what this movie dealt with—the reports of people who drove the trains, unloading the passengers at their grim destinations, and immediately robbing them of what they had brought with them as emergency rations. There were SS people and also a few longtime prisoners whose job it was to herd the new arrivals into the camps, robbing them of whatever they had brought with them, only to be robbed in turn by the camp capos. Then they were waiting for the next train to arrive, full of people, some of them sick with typhoid fever, starving, and driven by a preternatural craving to survive, in which everything moral totally breaks down.

But this wasn't the only horrendous thing shown in detail. There were people interviewed who lived around there and claimed they didn't know much of anything that had happened in the camps.

Everywhere there was evidence of gross denial and self-protection. And then, finally, at the end of this nine-hour horror show—and enormous research apparently went into the making of it—the filmmaker was interviewing a very liberal-minded American journalist and essayist who mostly blamed the Germans for what had transpired. There was not the slightest suggestion to look into ourselves, to question deeply and maybe find out how incidents such as those portrayed could actually be perpetrated by human beings like you and me, human beings as soulful, as refined, and as culturally genteel as many of the Germans were who were also shown and interviewed. None of us can really get around the question: How was this possible?

What would I have done had I lived around there, or had I known some of the leading figures in this horror show? Not shy away from this all-important question but ask it with a truly compassionate concern for all those suffering human beings. There was no probing into that. This was an amazing deficiency in this fantastically put-together nightmare of a movie. Somehow it remained shallow and biased. It did not try to encompass all humankind, whose latent potential is to fall into such traps— blind pitfalls—unless a thorough awakening takes place to our conditioning, our dormant potential to be programmed over and over again in such horrendously inhuman ways.

How many of us could believe that what Hitler and others proclaimed could be so resonant today, when people believe un-questioningly and unhesitatingly whatever the current U.S. ad-ministration declares to the public. Now there are some voices being heard expressing doubt and dissent, but right after 9/11 there was little or no dissent. No one dared to question much of anything. An erroneous connection was immediately established between the disasters in the U.S. and the leadership in Iraq. It was so reminiscent of what we had lived through in Germany— millions of flags flying all over the place, people feeling inspired and safe, connected with each other through flag waving—and thinking of war. Was this America? Or was this still Germany? Human beings everywhere asleep, adream with stories, distor-tions of the brain.

It's a good thing, a very good thing, when we get upset with something horrible that is happening not to squash the upset but to investigate. Investigate not just the *incident* we're so upset over but also *our own upset*. Is it genuine? Genuine horror at what hap-pened? Genuine compassion? Or is the you-versus-me syndrome alive and active to the extent that I cannot look at myself and everything is projected onto the other?

When we get upset, can we question why we get upset? Is there something going on in me that I don't want to acknowledge, or that I can't even see yet? But I can ask the question, live the ques-tion. Then, in that willingness and openness, things will reveal themselves, maybe to our total amazement. This can happen when there is openness and real curiosity about the ground of human misery, when there is curiosity without blame. Blame im-mediately stifles the probing. It projects a picture story—the story

of whom to blame and punish—onto the screen that is also my defensive wall. But I don't want a protective wall; I want everything
to be out in the open for inspection.

When the South Africans finally unearthed a lot of the horrors
that had been going on unacknowledged in their country, they
created a new institution called a "truth commission." And they
named this process "reconciliation." It was a wonderful new way
of approaching the situation. Not find out whether we have to
blame the culprits, kill them, hang them, but wonder seriously
whether there can be truth and reconciliation. The truth not
about these "terrible people," but about *all of us*. With that comes
inevitable reconciliation, because we are all of one common root.

I remember when the Americans took over Leipzig, the city
where I spent my childhood. My sister and I applied for jobs with
the American military government because we knew English very
well, and we immediately got hired as interpreters. One day I was
present when they had caught one of the most blatant Jew-haters
of Leipzig. I had only heard about him indirectly. But here he was
in the same room as me, shivering and afraid. And I had a strong
desire to see him really suffer, imagining myself saying something
threatening to him, like "Now we are going to do to you what you
did to us. It's only fair. It's justice." I recall this amazing thirst for
revenge being right there in myself. I also remember a woman
whose daughter had been gassed in Auschwitz—she was interviewed after Dr. Mengele, the camp physician who experimented
on prisoners, had been brought out of hiding. She said she didn't
want Mengele just to be killed, she wanted him "to suffer endlessly." And her face—she was actually a beautiful woman—her
face was horribly distorted, the beauty gone in the wake of feelings
of hatred and her need for revenge so that "justice may be done."
I felt very sorry for her. There was no release of reconciliation.

You could say that maybe there shouldn't be, *can't* be, reconciliation with somebody who has done something so horrible as
Dr. Mengele. But no—don't ever say from the outset that some-

thing is impossible. Nothing is impossible. The state of this body-mind can change in an amazing way. But not through willful intention. You can't just say, "I intend not to have this urge for gruesome revenge." It seems to be programmed into the cells of the body. True change has to arise in an entirely new state of openness, an openness in which there can be a release of old patterns—a release that has nothing to do with ego intention, with judging right and wrong, with precepts and virtue. It is the spontaneous leaving behind of all that to make room for something much vaster: TOTALLY UNINVITED LOVE.

part four

THIS ILLNESS, PAIN, AND DEATH

23

A Beautiful Mind

You notice the inner movement of wanting to be loved, and that's the reason you try to stick to the rules. Or, if you think you've transgressed, you feel guilty, constantly worrying whether you've done something wrong. If the pattern is seen, then the pattern is replaced with the seeing. Not doing something about it, because that would be creating another pattern. Just the openness of presence—wind blowing, quietly breathing in and out, in and out—simple, total presence. A constantly fresh replacement of the patterns with pattern-free being here, seeing, awaring.

Toni Packer: Someone wrote me the following note about my comments yesterday on the movie *A Beautiful Mind*. "Sorry to tell you, but that movie *A Beautiful Mind* is romanticized. I read the book, too, and also heard Nash being interviewed on the radio. It's an amazingly good movie. The book itself wouldn't have made a good movie at all." Signed "so-and-so."

If "so-and-so" wants to reveal herself . . . is it OK to ask what the motive was for writing this note? Did you feel that Toni was taken in by a romanticized movie, taking fabrication for truth? Actually I don't think that this was the case. This movie's story could have been totally invented—and still it doesn't matter. What matters is that something very special was created, something rooted in the depth of a human life story. I saw the interview 60 *Minutes* had with John Nash, which included a discussion with Nash, script-writer Ron Howard, actor Russell Crowe, and also Nash's wife, Alicia. It lent some "reality" to the movie.

When he was asked what it was like to come out of the siege of madness, John Nash replied that it was like waking up from a heavy nightmare. What was captured in the movie and the inter-views reminded me of two very close women friends who were stricken with similar paranoid schizophrenia years ago. One of the friends took her life, and the other one submitted to many courses of shock therapy.

The heartrending essence captured in this movie was that no matter how obscure, absurd, and seemingly insoluble the overlay of illusions and hallucinations may be, there remains the possibil-ity for a transformation happening in the brain—the possibility of waking up to a presence that is whole and undisturbed. In the movie it happened when Alicia, kneeling in front of John's bed, gently touches his cheek and whispers, "Is *this* real?"

Isn't this the essence of the work of this moment, discerning the difference between what is real and what is fantasy? There was beauty in showing that Nash no longer tried to "get rid of" hallu-cinations, hearing voices, and so on—allowing such symptoms to come and go on their own. He would simply say something like this: "I see some people over there looking at us and I hear voices in my head, but they're not *real* and need not be given any atten-tion. I don't have to do that anymore." The brain grew increas-ingly capable of ignoring perceptions of what was not real. In this development his wife, friends, and colleagues played an important part as a loving presence, continuing to ask, when needed, "Is this real or is it just imagination?" It is exceedingly helpful and impor-tant for all of us to ask questions like this once there has been an initial waking up from our lifelong dream-stories.

After another moment of great despair Alicia says to John, "I have faith that something extraordinary can happen." He heard her—her deep faith communicated itself. Whether this is simply the creation of a Hollywood scriptwriter or whether it really happened doesn't matter, does it? It addresses something that is possible to manifest in human beings at the depth of delusion and despair.

PARTICIPANT 1: I will reveal myself [*laughing*] as the one who wrote that note! And you're right, I didn't write it because I thought you would be taken in by romanticism. Your story of the two friends is really why I wrote it. Learning to discern what is real and what isn't doesn't always happen. I was married to a man who was bipolar and did not admit it. When I saw the movie, I was with some very good friends who had known both him and me. By that time he was dead; he had killed himself. The part in the movie where they tell her that he's crazy made me really weep, because no one ever diagnosed my husband or told me. So I was dragged into his hell for quite a long time. I would try to be clear and loving, but I never knew what was true. I was really involved in trying to make a normal life—we have two kids, and they seem to be very healthy—but it was only after he died that I took up meditation and saw the power of the overlay, the confusion. It was really clear that that's what killed him. That's what impelled me to inquire as strongly as I have. To not get so confused, to not have the confusion lead me to awful actions, especially one as awful as killing oneself. This month is the anniversary of his birth and his death, so it's an intense time. There were a lot of similarities between him and John Nash. And a very different outcome—to a great extent I felt like a failure. I really wanted it not to happen. So the balance between the possibility of waking up, helping another to do that . . . I have to balance that with the fact that it doesn't always work, either for yourself or for someone else you are trying to help. That's what was happening when I wrote the note. I was trying to hold both the possibility and also the fact that we don't control it.

TONI: You don't think it was made up that John Nash pulled out of this?

PARTICIPANT 1: No, I don't. But what disturbed me—I think it was revealed in an interview I heard with him that his son is schizophrenic, and he felt that his son wasn't working hard enough to see the unreality of *his* delusions. And I thought, "Whoops, that's it; that's the mistaken notion that you can do this by thinking your way out of it."

TONI: That's what Nash was trying to do himself, right? He suffered, screamed with frustration, because his was such a powerful problem-solving mind, saying, "I can solve this. I'll be able to solve this." But then came the realization that this was not solvable by thinking, but by thinking giving up trying. Thinking falling silent. When that happens, love reveals itself on its own.

It's what we're talking about here and inquiring into all the time. And people ask, "When the compulsion to figure things out through thinking drops away, can it drop away for good? Can this 'me,' this illusory network stop forever?"

No! But you can *see* it for what it is. You see that it's not *real* provided that at this moment there's the openness of seeing. There may be times when you don't *want* to see the futility of "me"-engagement—thinking about being praised and flattered—because it is very pleasurable! When the "me"-image gets hurt, well, then there is a motive for dropping it.

PARTICIPANT 2: It's amazing: What makes us certain about what is real and what is unreal? For instance, some simple thing comes to mind and immediately there's the decision that this is a memory, not a fantasy. Something made that jump. What do you think did that? We have this clear idea. We're totally sure that this is memory. But if our brain is not giving us correct information, has put this in the wrong place, saying it's a memory of something experienced in the past when in truth it is pure fantasy—well, we can nevertheless feel certain it's a memory. But if I'm here, truly present, then I can observe it. Or rather, it's directly seen that something is pure fantasy. *I'm* not doing that. How is this happening, that this amazing brain is doing that?

Toni: Something has to happen in the brain to be able to say with actual certainty "this is memory." Only when the brain is really clear and quiet can it say that. When it's not clear and quiet, it can say the wrong thing. It can say this is memory when it's fantasy or vice versa. That's the seemingly tricky thing. This is why we can't just argue with someone. We have to first stop the argument and get quiet.

Participant 2: But that depends on the healthy functioning of the brain. But with schizophrenia . . .

Toni: Krishnamurti said over and over until his dying day that there has to be a reasonably healthy brain (and organism) to see the false as false and the true as true. In order not to remain doggedly convinced that an illusion is the real thing, like the illusion of a separate "me."

But you cannot declare a brain "sick forever" just because it is not healthy for the time being. This is the beautiful thing about what happened to John Nash. There was this possibility of seeing the unreality of something, in spite of heavy hallucinations . . . and in spite of a brain that was working constantly, in his case working on pattern recognitions. He couldn't watch a bunch of pigeons pecking at crumbs without jotting down in what pattern they were eating. It was the obsession of this brain to figure out patterns and to put everything into formulas. And yet that brain healed to the point where he could teach properly again. He did good work. Wonderful. I think it's marvelous. [*pause*] And if it doesn't happen to me or you, then it doesn't; and you may end up taking your life because you don't want *this* one, but life goes on nonetheless. I'm not saying that callously, it's a fact.

Participant 3: This reminds me of the night before I came here, when I had dinner with a young man I've known and worked with for quite a while, who regularly had episodes of distress, threatening to kill himself, and had already been to see every therapist and psychiatrist in the book. He also has a frantic mother, who is on just as many medications as he is and who also has just as many therapists and psychiatrists. I've known these folks for seven or eight years now. I had taken him out to dinner because he'd dared to go to school again that day; it was a big celebration. I drove three hours to have dinner with him. He was sitting across from me and he was telling me absolutely fabulous lies—about what he was capable of doing and being. And yet every once in a while he'd take a bite of something delicious, really tasting it, and he'd say, "This really tastes good!" Or he'd have some kind of glancing comment about something that was *really* happening, and he'd look at me with his whole face open. I realized that the only thing that really was true, that was important there, was that we were eating together and that we were talking and that I could listen to him, and it didn't matter whether what he told me was true or false. He was this *being* that was there. And I could see him whole, even though he had this crazed, wild energy. You could see it in his face, all the clarity that was in there somewhere. So now you're talking about this cloud that can come over us, how we can suffer over so much of what happens with people we love . . . yet there is also this very simple thing. Whenever I get a chance, I just invite him to my house. He lies on the sofa, and the dog lies on his chest, and that's all there is.

TONI: And, you know, to finish with the story of the woman who *did* take her life, she came to say good-bye to me, though she didn't tell me she was going to take her life. Seeing her as I sat on the upper floor and she came up the stairs, I was surprised at how light she looked. Beautiful. And we had a wonderful conversation. Much more intimate than usual, for she was usually evasive and talked about how hopeless everything was. Then, as she went down the stairs, she turned and looked back up with a wordless "good-bye," and it was simple presence. Downstairs she chatted with the receptionist, which she normally didn't since she disliked meeting and interacting with people. This time she had already decided to put an end to it. So I never could grieve for her in the way you do when somebody is run over by a car.

PARTICIPANT 1: That shows, among other things, that the decision was taking control. It is often like that. And also, when people start taking medication or start having more energy, then that's a place of danger when it comes to suicide, because then they have the energy to make that decision.

TONI: But this woman never took medication. . . .

PARTICIPANT 1: Yes, it can happen on its own. It's that upswing of energy that leads to being able to take some control, but not enough control to be with the pain.

PARTICIPANT 4: The story you were telling triggered a memory of my mother. She died of a brain tumor. There was a point at which she understood that she was going to die and she decided not to take any more treatment. She had always been pretty tense and tried so hard to be good, to be careful about how she ate, and so on. I remember the relief on her face when she realized she was going to die. She had a box of chocolates sitting there and she said, "I can eat these and really enjoy them!" Those last few months were quite remarkable, because something freed up in her: the pressure of having to keep herself together to meet all those needs to be loved and be a good person. They softened for her, and so much more of her honest nature was released. It was really quite a poignant and amazing thing.

PARTICIPANT 1: I was just thinking how wonderful it would be to have those things release without death having to be imminent. I think that's part of why we're looking so hard at this "me"-structure, at the constraints that it puts on us.

PARTICIPANT 5: My father had severe dementia and came to live with me. Over a period of four years this overlay of "me" just deteriorated, and what showed up was radiant. He was so present that many people didn't know there was anything wrong with him. He was so perceptive, including perceptive about what was going on with other people. I would have conversations with him where I couldn't understand a thing he was talking about. It taught me to just be there, be present, but not try to use the mind to connect. I sometimes felt like I was in a transported state myself, because there was no way to stay intelligent with it in the usual way. After a conversation like this he would sometimes say, "That's it. That's conversation. The best conversation we've had!" He would call a bird "a fish" and . . . everything about it was topsy-turvy. It was so delightful to be with him. And when people would meet him, they'd see this radiant face.

After he passed away, many people said they'd never felt such love as they'd felt when meeting and greeting my father. Earlier in his life, when this overlay was there, he was judgmental, very prejudiced, hated some of my friends. I remember one friend who had dreadlocks. How my father hated him! But with the overlay gone, he greeted him with enthusiasm and delight, "Hey. My best friend is here!" So much was wonderful for him in the last years of his life. He enjoyed so much. Everything he ate was delicious; it didn't matter what it was. It was a powerful thing. It taught me so much about not needing to have so much mental construct to be very happy, present, free. So free. He had relatively good physical health, so he could do things. It was a very powerful thing to see. At his memorial service, when people spoke about their relationship with him—my brothers were there and also others who hadn't been willing to be around him during those last years— they were completely befuddled by what people who *had* been around him were saying about him.

PARTICIPANT 2: I heard many stories, especially when I was in India, of people becoming enlightened shortly before they died and I thought . . . well . . . the same as these stories some of you are telling point out to me: why wait? Whatever enlightenment is. I'm not saying I know what it is. But just to be with these people, what a gift.

PARTICIPANT 6: Why do we wait? Why can't we just . . . ? There must be a way. Why do we wait?

TONI: When you notice that you're waiting, ask immediately, "Why wait?"

PARTICIPANT 6: Krishnamurti said that you can step out of the overlay, out of the circle of blindness.

TONI: You're not even in it.

PARTICIPANT 6: But I seem to need someone else to show me that.

TONI: Years ago we had a man on staff here whose father had Alzheimer's. He would regularly go on visits to his father, and I would always get the report. These were often miserable visits because the father was so resentful about his sickness. He knew he had Alzheimer's and would ask, "Why me?" and on and on. And then one day this man came back from a visit and reported that his father no longer knew he had Alzheimer's. He said his father was free of burden, relieved of that knowledge that there was anything wrong with him. So I wonder, maybe people do not suffer as much as we project that they do, or maybe there is that kind of suffering but only in the initial stages, when they still want to function properly but realize they can't anymore. Eventually that passes as the part of the brain that keeps track of everything begins to deteriorate. What is there to keep track of except being here? The people here who have talked about their friends or relatives with Alzheimer's confirm that.

So can there be a shedding of this keeping track and judging ourselves now, while we're not sick? Of course, there are physical aspects to Alzheimer's too, aren't there? So it's not just a matter of mental deterioration.

[turning to Participant 5] Did your father have physical symptoms as well?

PARTICIPANT 5: No, not really. He was ninety-three when he died and was still quite robust. He knew that something was wrong with him, but he felt safe. So he didn't worry about it. Once he felt safe, he was OK with it. I sense that others with Alzheimer's who have maybe gone to institutions or have been in situations where other people try to control them more . . . they haven't done as well. I remember someone telling me that it didn't matter if my father put his shirt on over his pajama top, just worry about the big things. So once there was no longer any resistance there, he just enjoyed whatever was going on. He was like a child in that way. If he poured coffee on his cereal or whatever . . . and if I didn't make a thing out of it . . . then it was no problem for him. But if I made something out of it, he would be humiliated and then angry. I think he had a sense that he had a very safe place to be whatever he was. So there was no resistance. He talked to me sometimes about things he knew were wrong with him. He didn't know who I was, actually . . .

TONI: . . . and what does that matter? People make something out of that. But as long as there is a relationship . . .

PARTICIPANT 5: . . . exactly. If I just related, we were fine. But if I insisted on who I was, if the daughter in me came up and I insisted he relate to me as his daughter, it was very difficult for him. For both of us. But when I didn't care what he called me, and we were just two beings together there, then I was able to look after him and he knew and appreciated that.

TONI: In that way you had great value during this time he was going through.

PARTICIPANT 5: Also, I could tell the type of love he felt wasn't conditional on being father and daughter. I don't know how to describe it. It was open, not role based. He was very happy to relate to me, perhaps the way a small child would be. Not thinking the thought that "This person is taking care of me," but instead just being happy to be with someone who is caring.

PARTICIPANT 4: That sense of safety that your father felt where he poured coffee on his cereal but wasn't reprimanded for it . . . I'm thinking now about how painful it would have been for him to be in a situation where nothing he did fit the way he was supposed to be. Yet isn't that just how we all live? We have such a hard set of things that we're supposed to be doing . . . I suspect we don't know the half of it. And we do it to ourselves, mainly, and we do it to each other. So we don't feel safe. So all of those innocent ways that we are, that might come out wrong; we're so afraid and so careful. In my own world I think that's a very great sense of pressure, that lack of safety. And yet, when that's not taken too seriously, when those expectations are seen but somehow there's a softness around them, a good-heartedness, this is not such a big deal. Then a naturalness arises that's so much fun.

PARTICIPANT 1: This reminds me of a discussion at an earlier retreat where, [Participant 5], you brought up getting notes about smiling, from someone taking a kind of supervisory attitude. [*laughter*] I related to that, and was able to soften around it. I mean, I could see how I lay that kind of trip on myself, how we lay it on ourselves. For example, worrying about whether my clothes are too bright or am I walking too quickly . . . or whether my table manners are perfect. Seeing that this might just be a phase is helpful.

PARTICIPANT 7: But [Participant 4], you touched on something . . . this sort of persecutory inclination where we torment ourselves. . . .

PARTICIPANT 4: It's like . . . those rules are all there, those expectations . . . and following them, well, somehow it seems to be about getting love, that we'll be accepted, included, not judged. It's such an irony that you spend your life living in this rigid world of judgment, which is a world of rejection and separation, in order to be loved. It's a strange twist, isn't it?

TONI: [Participant 8] said this morning that we suffer from isolation, and isolate ourselves with this kind of behavior, with the judging, persecutory thoughts that the brain manufactures. So what can you do? See it, see it, see it. And stay in the seeing rather than the isolating stuff. That all comes and goes, but the seeing doesn't come and go in the same way. Can that seeing take the place of these absurd circuits?

PARTICIPANT 8: In seeing them, they show how absurd they are.

PARTICIPANT 4: And not adding to these circuits that we have to get rid of these judgments. That's just a new version of the same old story.

TONI: To see that without doing *anything* about it. Just listening to the fan—not intentionally but because it's there. That's really what it all amounts to—the replacement of these hyperactive, worrisome, wanting modes with quietness and presence, the one taking the place of the other. And not once and for all but all the time. Freshly.

PARTICIPANT 4: Could you speak about that replacement? I'm not sure I understand what you mean by that.

TONI: You had a very good example: You notice the inner movement of wanting to be loved, and that's the reason you try to stick to the rules. Or, if you think you've transgressed, you feel guilty, constantly worrying whether you've done something wrong. If the pattern is seen, then the pattern is replaced with the seeing. Not doing something about it, because that would be creating another pattern. Just the openness of presence—wind blowing, quietly breathing in and out, in and out—simple, total presence. A constantly fresh replacement of the patterns with pattern-free being here, seeing, awaring. But it's not a word. It's the absence of all these judgment patterns. Either stuck in the patterns or replacing stuckness with openness. Presence. That's not stuck. It just allows everything to come and go. It's not rigid with this anxiety of holding on. [*pauses*] Wanting to feel safe— this can be a stuckness also.

PARTICIPANT 9: And if you do feel safe, then wanting to do everything to keep that safety.

TONI: To keep it, yes. There's an assumption in there, which may be false. When there's freedom, there's no need for this patterned safety. We love repetition. And maybe we can't get along without it. I don't know. I find it's a relief to just for a moment be free of the pattern, and feel the wind, the breathing, the walking. Without a plan.

PARTICIPANT 2: You know, the word *replace* sounds a bit like taking the one and replacing it with the other. But, in truth, if you're stuck with something, it can open up that there's nothing to do and nothing to replace.

TONI: Well, let me look. [*pauses*] You're stuck, and you say, "It can open up." Well, what is this "it" that we say can open up? What is that really, other than awareness?

PARTICIPANT 2: When it opens up, it comes into awareness, but I'm not replacing something . . . .

TONI: No, no, I didn't mean it that way. This is the danger of words. There's no "replacer."

PARTICIPANT 2: It sounded so simple, to just replace the one—stuckness—with the other—openness.

TONI: Well, it *is* simple. But there's no doer in it. And the words, I'll grant you, are incomplete or insufficient. It's just . . . where this wanting was, it's not there anymore. Instead there is seeing, awaring, listening, sensing. Putting it in words, we say I replaced one with the other. Which does not do justice to this thing, which doesn't even take time, which is just the instantaneousness of seeing.

PARTICIPANT 2: When you mentioned the fan a couple of minutes ago, it so happens that I had just then caught myself very much engaged in thought. Then it opened up again. It happened. It was so clear that it just came . . .

PARTICIPANT 8: . . . and sometimes this opening up doesn't come: stuck, stuck, stuck!

[*much group laughter*]

TONI: How do you know that?

[*more group laughter*]

PARTICIPANT 8: It's not all the time. Everything happens. Including the stuckness.

PARTICIPANT 4: I'm still working with this notion of replacement . . . it feels . . . let me see if maybe we're saying the same thing in different ways . . . when there's movement into criticizing myself and the fear and clutching start to build . . . and the feeling is that it's within this field of presence that it's building, and somehow that brings goodheartedness, love—just that open spaciousness with it. And the judging and clutching don't continue to build in the same way. That stuff doesn't grab the body and take over. It subsides, and the spaciousness that was there all along remains.

TONI: Could we add awareness to it? Spacious awareness?

PARTICIPANT 4: Yes. It's the same.

TONI: The same indescribable—

PARTICIPANT 4: —poor words, in a way.

TONI: Yes. So what are we trying to clarify? We're not trying to clarify whether there's somebody who does it, because that's clear, isn't it? There is no doer in this thing. There's only awaring. And awaring has this seemingly magic function that what is *truly* awared changes, is no longer the same. Now, you can say, "Well, I'm aware, but the fear is still there." Well, then, what else is there? There are still thoughts running that sustain the fear or add fresh fear, because without thoughts, memories—whether mental or physical—there is no fear. Without anything dividing, there is no fear.

So, [Participant 4], are we together on this, or . . .

PARTICIPANT 4: Yes, I think we are. The different words that I was using don't sound different than what you were describing.

TONI: It isn't different. If we're both looking at the same thing, words don't matter so much. Some words help some people more than others. And they can also do mischief—romanticize something, for example.

PARTICIPANT 5: With this intensive noticing . . . I remember once, Toni, you talked about seeing fear begin to arise and then just not going with it because there is so much room around it. You can have something that ordinarily would be gripping, easily stuck to, growing and filling up the space—but you just don't go with it. In the same way that the surface of the pond just gets smooth again after the breeze has stirred it up a bit. The environment that we're in here at retreat, at Springwater, has so many fewer stimuli in it, so you can see this stuff start to arise and actually not go along with it. Or see the inclination to go along with it rather than wake up to it after you've already gone off with it.

TONI: Yes. Yes. See the inclination to go with it, and there's still the energy *not* to go because it's seen to be futile.

PARTICIPANT 9: I think that how fast we see anything that's arising will depend on how strong the conditioning is—when it's stronger, it takes more room to see it. If the conditioning to react with anger is very strong, there can be some looking at that conditioning, but it is still running. There is some space, but this conditioning is dominant, you know? So it takes time to sustain this staying here, the energy to stay here.

TONI: The energy of staying here has to be stronger than the energy of the anger, or whatever the reaction.

PARTICIPANT 9: Yes. That's it.

TONI: And the energy of anger is mixed with all kinds of ingredients, including the pleasure of being angry. I'm taking that as an example, but there are other things in there: you *want* to be angry, you have a *right* to be angry, the other person *deserves* a piece of our mind . . . our beautiful mind . . . . [*much group laughter*]

24

What Is Dying?

A lot of upset with the death of somebody very close to us is linked to fear about our own living and dying, isn't it? "How will I live on without him?" "I miss him terribly." "How will I die when my time comes? Will it be a painful, drawn-out death? I will no longer be here to see the morning sunrise over the hills"—all this thinking, imagining, and remembering, with painful emotions stirring.

QUESTIONER: I'm not sure how to ask this, so I'll just say what's coming up. My dad died recently. I was very close to him. There was a moment a few days before he died at sunset in bed at home and we were talking. Our eyes met, and in that glimpse, selfing fell away. He wasn't he, and I wasn't I; something was transcended. Then we went right back in. It was like this moment, and, ah, it was very powerful, when I think of it. There was peace—like a gift, one of his parting gifts, I felt. And uh, then he died. I watched his coffin being lowered into the ground, and my mind got numb. . . .

And so I'm not sure what my question is, but just that someone you've known for forty-one years doesn't exist on the planet anymore in the form you knew him. It feels like the biggest loss ever. I don't know if I even have a question or if I want to just let it pop out and see what comes from you about that.

Toni Packer: Right now, this very moment of looking-listening together, where is your father?

Questioner: It seems like a pile of memories, and thoughts and sensations.

Toni: Yes, yes, and then there's the moment when there was no selfing. At that moment, was he even your father?

Questioner: No.

Toni: Is this what he is right now—this present moment without "father" or "daughter?" Simple being.

[*pause*]

But does this immediately become a comforting thought, something to hold on to again?

So what was he really? The one you remember being close to for forty-one years—many, many different memory images over many years—or the one dying, the one in the lowered casket? Before he was born, what was your father?

[*pause*]

See, we get overpowered by thoughts and feelings that evolve out of a sad or a happy story. That's really the biggest tearjerker, isn't it? I am not making fun of your situation.

On the last day of retreat, I read old and contemporary masters and poems. There is one by Mary Oliver called "Boston University Hospital." Does anybody know that? It's a beautiful poem. A couple of times when I read it, I choked up. When my husband was ill, that poem just made me choke. It's about a dear friend recovering right next to where someone else has died. I haven't read it recently, because I don't want to choke up reading a poem. Without that poem, where are the tears? I am not saying tears are unnecessary or shouldn't come up—just to listen silently and to wonder about it all.

A lot of upset with the death of somebody very close to us is linked to fear about our own living and dying, isn't it? "How will I live on without him?" "I miss him terribly." "How will I die when my time comes? Will it be a painful, drawn-out death? I will no longer be here to see the morning sunrise over the hills"—all this thinking, imagining, and remembering, with painful emotions stirring.

In silent listening, inwardly, there can be a wondrous illumination of the conditioned, reactive bodymind. It gets more and more transparent with sustained awareness. And yet one easily gets entangled in what reveals itself—the desires, the fears, all the emotional-physiological states connected with memory and anticipation. All of it has such an amazingly powerful attraction, seriously masquerading for the real thing. Entanglement in what presents itself is instant movement away from simple luminous presence, like entering a dark playhouse with its enchanting lights.

Right at this moment, can we see our life story permeated with awareness? Beholding it quietly in the midst of breathing and throbbing. It's not necessary to continue with the involvement in story and emotion, no matter how strongly and convincingly the body vibrates with memories. Can there be a simple shift from story-entanglement to open listening, this moment? In this there is no fear of passing away. Coming and going is happening in vast emptiness without limitation, without time. It's the ego-playhouses that produce all the shows of love and hatred, fun and horror, pain and pleasure, in artificial light. Fathers, husbands, mothers, babies—coming and going, coming and going, coming and going—timeless presence. Love without fear.

25

Helping Those in Pain

I think one of the greatest remedies or help that can happen to us is if somebody really listens to us—and also gives us some indication that they are listening, some feedback.

A PERSON HERE WHO is a psychotherapist has clients who not only have tremendous mental, psychological pain but great physical pain, enormous physical pain. She says, "I don't know what to do about that. Not being a doctor, not being able to refer or prescribe, not even knowing much about medicines, I don't know . . . . What am I to do?" I really felt with this person. What are we to do when our job is to help somebody with enormous pain and we don't know what to do for this person, how to relieve that? I mentioned maybe to have the client pay attention to the breathing, and she said, "Yes, I do that, but then the client says that when she goes home, the attention is gone again."

Well, we all have that problem, that it's not the same at home as when we sit here together in a quiet, bright, empty hall surrounded by beautiful meadows and woodlands. So not to overextend yourself, thinking that you can also help this person at home. Take it here, right here and now where you meet with each other. And if you are able, don't just say, "Watch your breathing," but breathe together. You sit there and you breathe, audibly demonstrating it in yourself, really *with* your breath, and maybe something will be resonating in that other person and they will join in. How long it will last, well, we don't know.

But then later, after our discussion, another thing occurred to me. As you may know, I am at times going through indescribable pain. I have medications and pain doctors and injections—which help for a certain period of time—but nothing helps completely, and there the pain is again. Then I go to a doctor, a neurologist, or pain specialist, and I have only found one who has really listened and done something. Most of them write endlessly in their books. But nothing has come of it, and I feel they haven't understood me. So I talk about it again, feeling maybe I should make it clearer. With one doctor, I see the assistant first, and I have to tell her how I have been in the last quarter of a year, and then she disappears for a while. She tells the neurologist and he tells me his conclusions from what his assistant told him about what she heard from me. What has been relayed to him never seems complete, so then I describe it to him again. I get exhausted in the process and very frustrated.

I think one of the greatest remedies or help that can happen to us is if somebody really listens to us—and also gives us some indication that they are listening, some feedback. Because if somebody just writes things down and remains stone-faced, then you think, "Well, I didn't put it clearly enough." So play with that, to see whether you can listen to these patients and give back to them what you have understood in a real empathetic way—and not just to pretend, because as a patient you are very sensitive whether a person comes from a compassionate, empathetic place or whether they just have a routine. Sometimes the assistants say, "I really feel sorry for what you have to go through." This is usually said in a way that means "good-bye," and you don't want to hear that; it's not relevant. You want to be understood.

I think many of you will agree that it is balm to the wounds when somebody listens to us and understands us. We are not even asking for advice; we just want to be heard. Maybe that diminishes

the burden already, so we don't have to talk to ourselves, or pre-
pare for telling yet another person for whom understanding never
seems to happen. We can drop it a bit.

Of course, I did ask the psychotherapist who is here whether
she herself has experienced a lot of pain, and she hasn't. If you
have, you are in a very good position to share things that you are
not in a position to share when you haven't gone through pain.
But not to expect that of oneself, because then it easily becomes
hypocritical. Still, some people, without having gone through
something themselves, have that amazing sensitivity to enter into
somebody else's state and feel it and convey that feeling.

26

Illness and the Self

With illness one's deeply ingrained identity as a healthy, physically capable person does not hold up any longer, and that hurts. Thoughts and images do cause hurt and pleasure, don't they? A collapsed self-image smarts, not just mentally but physically.

SOMEONE WROTE TO ME in a letter, "Since my present illness I have come to realize that illness easily brings one back to a conventional notion of self. There is this feeling that 'obviously' I am the one who is ill. Referring to us both, *you* are ill in your own 'individualized' way, and *I* in mine."

For a while now I have intended to write something about illness, but it didn't occur to me "that illness easily brings one back to the notion of self." My first reaction to this statement was, "Why just illness?" Don't the notions of "me" and "you," "mine" and "yours" permeate our entire life? And isn't it an unquestioned assumption that this "me"-self *is* my body? Or rather, that I am my body and mind? I have *my* ill body, not yours. You have yours, which isn't mine. Each of us can only feel our own pain, not the other person's. My body distinguishes me from you, in sickness and in health. This is how we think, isn't it?

Did you mean that having to deal with illness creates more self-consciousness than being well? Why would it? Would it be because we become more self-conscious when things aren't the way they used to be?

Comparing myself with others may be an important factor in this, as in "He is in much better shape than I am," or "She is even worse off than I am." I heard on the radio that a woman in her nineties is a champion weight lifter! Wow! Comparison with one's own incapacity arises instantly. And then the thought: "I was so healthy in the past, hiked in the mountains, and skied downhill—where has it all gone?" Remembered images like these can plague the bodymind!

With illness one's deeply ingrained identity as a healthy, physically capable person does not hold up any longer, and that hurts. Thoughts and images do cause hurt and pleasure, don't they? A collapsed self-image smarts, not just mentally but physically. We become anxious, worried, sentimental, self-pitying, forced to live in an unaccustomed and undesirable story about ourselves. A story we do not like. It does not fit us, as we know ourselves. We may even feel embarrassed or ashamed about our sickness, resulting in more agony.

Where is all this self-involvement coming from? Do we really feel that we were less self-involved *before* falling ill? Look at it: hasn't the old self-image of being a healthy, active, vigorous person (in which there may have been considerable pride) just given way to a new one of being sick, disabled, or even an invalid, which literally means "in-valid"? These images hurt as much as the earlier ones pleased and made us feel great. Our world has changed.

Now, you could say, "Wait a minute! It's not just the self-image that has changed. The whole body has changed in a painful, unpleasant way." Yes, you are right—it has: we can't do what we used to do; we are becoming dependent on others, maybe even helpless without them. These are all undeniable facts that need a lot of getting used to—having to learn new routines because the old ones simply do not work any longer. It is a jolt to the organism—the loss of old routines to which there had been psychological as well as physical attachment.

At the same time we may become aware of the astounding resourcefulness of this bodymind to adjust to new conditions. Also illness may bring about a humility never before tasted, and a genuinely felt compassion with people in pain. Realizing our common vulnerability. How fragile we human beings are—so easily perishable!

I am questioning again whether changes in our state of health need to be translated into imagery and story line. We do seem to prefer living in stories about ourselves to being in direct touch with the facts of our changing condition. There is considerable attachment to our stories for better or worse, isn't there? It's an amazing discovery.

It is true that pain and disability are difficult to endure. Even without any story spun around them, the body endeavors to rid itself of pain or to ameliorate it in any way possible. This is a natural impulse in animals as well. So we do what we can to feel better: see doctors, take medications, read books, go to movies, watch TV, see friends, or go for walks if we can. But does any of this necessitate making a story about "you" as a separate being from "me"? *That* is where self-consciousness is born and thrives—in story and image—not in the bare facts of illness itself.

Can we ask freely whether stories about the suffering "me" are necessary for living? Do we realize how entangled and vulnerable we are on account of them? How additional physical discomfort arises from feeling sorry for ourselves?

Being free of illness does not mean being free of self-consciousness. Only *awareness* this present moment frees—in illness and in health. Awareness replaces thinking and fantasizing about myself with simply being here—computer humming, keyboard clicking, wind rattling, snowmelt dripping, heart beating, back paining, breathing in and out, in and out—one moment at a time.

27

Letter to a Deceased Friend

Remember the time I overcooked the Brussels sprouts to the point of complete nonrecognition, and you felt that you had never tasted anything more delicious?

Dearest Jeanie,

Instead of writing something "about" you and our long, deep friendship, it feels so much more natural to address you directly, right here by the hum of the computer! Even though the thinking mind knows that you as a living flesh-and-blood friend are no longer with us, the joyous memory of goodness and love radiating from your whole being comes to life the instant I think of you! Yes, Jeanie, memory pictures and feelings do have truth and aliveness all their own in that they can kindle loving presence and wonder in the silent beholder. I'm sure that you would know what I'm talking about if you were on the other end of the phone right now—our frequent way of communicating with each other when we could not be physically together in the same place.

I don't precisely recall the day we met in North Tonawanda in the late sixties—only that there was an immediate understanding that the best we could do was sit together in silence. We had a little basement *zendo* that grew in participation and Zen accoutrements over the many years we spent there. Now and then we stayed there together overnight for *sesshins* of several days, or met during the daytime for a morning sitting and a friendly lunch together. Remember those lunches? You would bring the world's most precious cheeses, Joe brought bread, and I cooked a soup. Remember the time I overcooked the Brussels sprouts to the point of complete nonrecognition, and you felt that you had never tasted anything more delicious? "You must give me that recipe!" you exclaimed. (It never turned out that well again, probably because the original hadn't been made according to any intentions!)

We shared together not only our regular sitting time and group *dokusans* but all the happy and troubling events of our two small family households. Something worrisome or difficult was always taking place, to be shared, thought about, temporarily despaired over, or allowed to be left alone in mutual not-knowing—that dark womb of daily being that can give birth to amazing patience, and eventually, to fresh insights—or just the quieting down and withering away of unnecessary concerns.

In spite of initial resistance and hesitancy, you eventually went to a few small retreats at the Rochester Zen Center, but happily joined the Genesee Valley Zen Center (now Springwater Center) when some of us left to start a new center away from tradition. Your nature seemed too gentle and vulnerable to fit the stark Zen requirements, and you never wavered in your decision to join Springwater Center. Your love for silence and the absence of constricting forms and schedules as well as your deep understanding of the wisdom of simple presence without ego were the inner beacon that guided your often conflicted personal life.

One time during a retreat where participants could sign up to give talks, you suddenly sat down on the mat near the door (you had hardly taken the time to write your name on the schedule) to give a talk you knew not about what. So far the retreat talks and group dialogues had splashed about the surface of things without diving into the source and depth of our confusion. If I remember right, in your gentle, quiet voice you questioned un-waveringly if we could ever detect the ego with its immense self-defenses and protection that keep us from seeing clearly what we are thinking and doing. It was a very short talk, which made its point in the simplest manner without any personal neediness blocking the flow. There was no disturbing "listen to me" projec-tion—on the contrary. The talk flowed out of pure no-"me," illu-minating the "me" in all its gross and subtle ways.

Later you told me that you didn't know what moved you with such certainty and equanimity to give that talk except the strong need to clarify confusion—all shyness and feelings of insufficiency that you tended to suffer from so much had disappeared.

Years later when I asked you if you would like to carry on the Springwater work when Toni had passed away, you immediately said, "Yes, Toni, this is my life." But hours or days later, when the usual doubts arose, you wondered if you could ever do it—that timid Jeanie, conditioned to be modest, self-effacing, self-doubting, tried to take over again! It didn't take long to see the shadow play for what it was and to drop it with the clarity of under-standing: of course the "I" can't "do" it, but, as in that retreat, won-drous action takes place when the "doer" is quiet.

It's quiet now, dearest Jeanie, completely quiet. All illusive separation has ceased to be.

With an embrace in love,
Toni

28

Suffering
and Awareness

An Interview with Toni Packer
by Geoff Swaebe

The instant you come upon the ocean of awareness that is always here, and the energy is gathering in it naturally, effortlessly, there is nothing that can stress or bother you.

GEOFF SWAEBE: Do you ever experience anxieties that awaken you at night?

TONI PACKER: Oh yes! That can happen.

GEOFF: And in those moments do you meditate on the source of that worry or anxiety?

TONI: If I really have a problem or unfinished business that agitates the mind, it may be helpful to get up from bed and sit, allowing the stirred-up organism to settle down. But that can also happen while staying in bed, quietly wondering what is really going on, what is upsetting. Let the knot show itself in all its twists and turns and disentangle itself in quiet, patient wondering and attending.

I don't experience these things happening so often anymore

because knotty problems that are encountered during the day aren't left very long to fester from inattention. When I get upset over something, I usually pause, quiet down, and listen inwardly. Let the situation reveal itself quietly. Is there something I can do about the matter right away, or can it wait until morning? Maybe just jotting down a note right then and there is helpful for the brain that wants order.

When I wake up during the night without being in the grip of a problem, it is important to learn not to make a problem out of needing to go back to sleep. Not giving way to disturbing thoughts that I need eight hours of sleep, that I won't be fresh enough in the morning, and so on. Let it be, let it be! Then there can be a shift in the mind from "efforting," from trying to go to sleep to relaxing quietly. Trying to get someplace other than where I am right now always goes together with resistance—the resistance to letting be what is! Just lying here quietly is altogether different from straining to go to sleep. Falling asleep happens on its own, just as waking up does! Neither can be forced.

GEOFF: One incentive for taking up meditation has to do with the fact that it can provide us with a way to work with nagging thoughts and to reduce stress or anxiety. Do you ever look at it as such?

TONI: I do not see that as its aim, but I don't quarrel with someone coming to Springwater who might have that incentive in mind. In deepening meditation, incentive falls away. It's not needed because true meditation is self-sustaining. It is totally sufficient unto itself.

When intelligent insight into what has been bothering me takes place, that thing can usually be recognized as no cause for alarm. With intelligent insight into a problem, the problem can abate. And with that comes stress reduction. The instant you come upon the ocean of awareness that is always here, and the energy is gathering in it naturally, effortlessly, there is nothing that can stress or bother you. Of course that state may not be immediately available when you've just come from the bustle of New York City or wherever you may live and work. So the first order of things is to sit with turbulence and not waste energy on wishing it would go away—that only creates more conflict and stress.

Perhaps we could say that meditative inquiry occasions natural stress reduction—learning not to be in conflict with thoughts and conditions but instead silently listening as the mind churns, feeling the unrest throughout the body without wishing it away. It is being present with all disquieting (or happy) thoughts and the total situation that spawns them. And the more you engage in meditative awareness and inquiry, the less resistance there is to what is happening: the pain, anxiety, anger, pleasure. They can freely come up when habitual resistance disappears.

But then you might think, "Oh no! Now I've got more thoughts and fears than ever before." OK! Let it be. It's all right! As it turns out, diminished resistance allows formerly suppressed thoughts to slip through. So—just to be here with what is, whether lots of thoughts or few, pleasant ones or disturbing ones. It's an opportunity to behold it all in silence. Then the bodymind can quiet down as the source of anxiety reveals itself. We want the image of ourselves to be loved, protected, admired, and accepted forever, and that insatiable demand spawns constant stress and conflict. Why keep expecting the impossible when it is possible to be fully with what is?

GEOFF: This reminds me of examples in literature . . . for example, when Parsifal asks the Grail King, "What torments thee?" Or in the New Testament when Christ asks the lame man at Bethesda, "Wilt thou be whole?"

TONI: What replaces torment with wholeness are not the words but the source whence these words issue.

GEOFF: In the speaker?

TONI: Yes. Yes. The question "Wilt thou be whole?" isn't just a matter of words. When the speaker is whole, undivided within himself and from the listeners, then the listeners may freely realize their own inherent wholeness. Parsifal . . . I don't know . . . he was said to have been raised by his fearful mother in total ignorance, a dumb fool raised without any worldly skills or knowledge. Maybe what is meant by that is an innocence that prevailed in place of a separate "me." It is in this innocence that he asks of the king, "What is ailing you?" And he receives the answer: "It is this wound." Can our wounds heal in the presence of a totally innocent question? Why not?

GEOFF: It's our suffering that leads us to ask these questions. Then can suffering be a catalyst for the "me" to begin a journey out of itself?

TONI: Yes, of course. Though it only appears like a journey. At the moment of waking up there is the realization that presence has never been away; it's always been here. In looking back you can describe your journey out of suffering, or by looking ahead you can project a journey out of it. But in truth, there is no journey. There is only being here—which leads nowhere, because it is everywhere. Everything is here, without time.

GEOFF: Some traditions try to explain egotism and the "me"-feeling in terms of a larger purpose, such as waking up. Would you go as far as to say that there is no waking up without the suffering caused by egotism?

TONI: It can be put more simply. When there isn't any painful entanglement in the sticky "me"-web, what do we need to wake up from? Often we just suffer along without even realizing that we are suffering. But then comes a moment of waking up to that state of sorrow and with it a wondering: "Why am I suffering? Is that all there is to my life? Is there any way out? Can suffering end?" That was the Buddha's question: "Why are human beings suffering, and can it come to an end?" It immediately set in motion for him a fresh wondering and watching, and out of that the awakening to wholeness that is without the sorrow of "me." The next thing is wanting with all one's heart to communicate to others what has been seen and understood.

But you have to be careful not to say something like, "If there was no suffering, there would be no awakening to presence." Or that suffering is "necessary" in order to awaken. I can see no reason to create extra suffering through spiritual training; there is enough suffering within every human being without needing to add more!

Simple listening without a listener (without habitual interpretations) is without error, whereas reacting out of strong habitual emotions is a constant source of error in our relationships. Right now this is going on and on with all the violent conflicts in the world. Can we see clearly what leads to what? Bombing the presumed "aggressor" leads to retaliation that leads to further violence. There is no beginning to that and no end. Violence leads to violent reaction. More bombing creates more hatred. More hatred spawns suicide bombing, which brings about more hatred. It's so clear! "Intelligent" looking and listening means seeing and deeply understanding the entire network of cause and effect—the Buddha called it the chain of becoming.

So, do we need suffering in order to wake up? No. There is a need to wake up to the fact of suffering! And with this come the questions "Does this have to continue?" "Is there any sense to this?" Let some fundamental questions arise out of waking up to our condition of being caught up in suffering, separation, enclosure, isolation. Then let the intelligence of awareness do its work.

part five

THIS LIVING,
LOVING WONDER

29

What Energizes
My Life?

So when you're walking outside under the open sky, the fresh breeze, rustling leaves, distant hills, birdcalls—is this in-touchness with "nature" a different kind of energy? [*pause*]

It's the energy of being completely present, and it's not generated by problem-solving impulses. Being totally present doesn't generate the "me"-circuit!

PARTICIPANT 1: It seems to me that this body is very much used to getting energized by trying to prevent bad things that have happened from repeating themselves—trying to make the future better. This problem-solving circuit seems to be feeding on itself so much that that's almost all I am! There isn't any space for anything else to come in. [*pause*]

TONI PACKER: Problem solving has its place.

PARTICIPANT 1: Yes. But getting one's energy for daily living from solving the problems of one's life is not—

TONI: What is the problem of one's life? [*group laughter*]

PARTICIPANT 1: [*laughing loudly*] I'm probably not even solving the *right* problems! I guess the question for me is: Where can energy come from if not from this self-concern with its compulsion to solve problems?

TONI: OK. Yes. The whole "me"-network *is* a powerful energy generator.

PARTICIPANT 1: Yes, it really gets me moving . . .

TONI: . . . moving in my conditioned patterns: to solve my problems, to succeed in life, to prevent failing, to get answers. Where is this whole movement coming from? What is the source of it? *That's* a good question!

PARTICIPANT 2: You know, I *think* I'm energized when I'm solving the problems of my life, but in looking more closely I find that I'm exhausted from it all. It takes so much energy and drains me . . . yet I'll even have resistance to sleep because I'm thinking there are so many problems to be solved! When I finally sleep, I wake up thinking about the problems again. So I may think I'm generating a lot of energy struggling with problems, but actually I'm *expending* it. But if I'm in one of these lucky places where I forget to solve problems [*laughs*]—like when I'm outside for a walk and the sounds and sights are just here—I don't feel that kind of exhaustion. If I'm physically tired, I can just go take a nap.

TONI: So when you're walking outside under the open sky, the fresh breeze, rustling leaves, distant hills, birdcalls—is this in-touchness with "nature" a different kind of energy? [*pause*]

It's the energy of being completely present, and it's not generated by problem-solving impulses. Being totally present doesn't generate the "me"-circuit!

You can ask, how does one know that? Well, I'm looking right now. Let's look and listen quietly. [*pause*]

Is there any "me"-circuit running this moment? Are there any thoughts like "I have to do . . . ," "I have to be . . . ," "I have to fix . . ."? No, there's nothing of that—no ego-generating movement can be detected. Yet this other unnamable energy is here.

And if a problem comes up, a problem that has to be solved, well, there is energy to deal with it.

PARTICIPANT 2: Often the problems I think I have to solve come from trying to maintain my notions of what's "good" or "kind" or how I should be, so I throw all those problems in with my professional ones. I mean, it's not an open questioning; it's an effoting kind of problem solving. That's when I'm the most exhausted, not when I'm trying to solve work problems. That also feels like energy—but not at all like the energy of being, just being.

TONI: Just being.

30

Is Enlightenment a Myth?

A Letter and a Reply

Enlightenment, True Nature, True Self, Wholeness, the Unconditioned Absolute—whatever words have been given to
what is without words, unthinkable, unknowable, ungraspable—is not the effect of a cause.

DEAR TONI,

I listened to your tape *Does Meditation Lead to Enlightenment?*
and, not getting satisfaction, I followed it up with *The Myth of Enlightenment* by Gangaji. I am still disappointed.

You spoke at length about this question, the motivations for
the question, and how the question applies to practice. Though
you go deeply into the question, neither you nor anyone else ever
seems to go deeply into the answer. Does meditation lead to enlightenment?

Why can't anyone come clean on this?

The fellow who asked this question of you was very honest
and vulnerable; his was not a query but a plaintive cry. He had
been at this for twenty or thirty years and had not gotten enlightened and wanted to know now, once and for all, does it happen? Is it going to happen? Does meditation lead or does it not

lead to enlightenment? Is it going to happen to *me*? Yes, *me*. This person.

. . .

Dear _____,

You write that though Toni and others go deeply into the question of whether meditation leads to enlightenment, no one seems to go deeply into the answer. "Why can't anyone come clean on this?" you ask in exasperation.

The reason for this is simply that enlightenment has no cause whatsoever. Enlightenment, True Nature, True Self, Wholeness, the Unconditioned Absolute—whatever words have been given to what is without words, unthinkable, unknowable, ungraspable—is not the effect of a cause. It is luminously present and timeless, overlooked by the roving intellect that is trying to grasp it and obscured by the bodymind's constantly shifting moods, desires, and fears. Moment-to-moment meditation is clearly coming upon this roving and shifting, resisting and fearing mind and the urge to do something about it! Pausing for an instant—is there any doer?

Meditation that is free and effortless, without goal, without expectation, is an expression of Pure Being that has nowhere to go, nothing to get.

As you know from experience, it's the hardest thing to be silently, motionlessly present, no matter what may be going on within this conditioned bodymind. Meditation reveals conditioning as conditioning, witnessing it quietly, with no need to move toward or away from it. Truth reveals itself on its own. It happens. Meditation reveals conditioning unconditionally.

This is all I can say for now. No need to go at it with force. As the German poet Goethe wrote in *Faust*, "What Nature doesn't reveal to you spontaneously, you cannot force from her with crowbars and screws." Meditation proceeds silently, without the aid of violent contrivances!

Can we let it unfold, quietly, without asking for anything?

31

The Observer
Is the Observed

It's not that *you* are open. No limitation. No borderlines. Yes.
If *you* want to *become* open, you're in trouble!

PARTICIPANT 1: Sometimes when I get very agitated, I go out to
the path behind the house and start walking. As I go up that path,
part of me is saying, "I'm not even going to notice the leaves and
the light because I'm so agitated, distracted!" But then I keep
walking anyway, though there are more thoughts telling me,
"Damn! I'm having this internal conversation again. Why can't I
just be here?" I'm getting angry at myself now. But I just keep
walking, go up the hill and down, and the agitation starts to peter
out. There's more light and leaves.

TONI PACKER: And suddenly you realize you're in a different
state?

PARTICIPANT 1: Yes.

PARTICIPANT 2: For me, whenever agitation and stuckness get
really painful and there is no openness, there come thoughts about
"*me* having them," a me who *has* this painful stuckness. Following that, thoughts arise that I shouldn't be having this pain, I
should be more advanced than this, or whatever. But if I'm able
to see that the observer *is* the observed, only then is it possible—

as Toni pointed out—to "be with it." Which means there is no one *having* anything—there is just seeing "I" am that pain now —nothing different from that. Just seeing "this is what is now." "The observer is the observed." This is not my sentence—Krishnamurti put it like this, and you too, Toni, have said it. Sometimes when I'm really stuck, it helps quite beautifully to remember this sentence.

TONI: So at that moment the statement really means something to you! I am wondering, what's the difference between having an "intellectual understanding" and a sentence acting upon us directly? It sounds like you're talking about something that is deeper than the level of "intellectual understanding."

PARTICIPANT 2: Yes. There's a switch . . .

TONI: And you don't need to feel sorry for yourself anymore. That self-pity is all gone.

PARTICIPANT 2: Well, everything negative is activated when I'm in that stuckness—suffering, self-pity, pain about my life, what I've done wrong, my failures, my inability to do anything— all that is activated. When direct contact with all of that happens, then there is just the rain, the birds. There is more space around. Openness.

TONI: It's not that *you* are open . . .

PARTICIPANT 2: There's . . . opening . . .

TONI: No limitation. No borderlines. Yes. If *you* want to *become* open, you're in trouble! [*chuckles*]

PARTICIPANT 3: So then even the watcher comes into awareness—the whole "me"-network comes into view. As you say, the observer is the observed. The one who is observing *is* this hidden "me"-network—hidden until it, too, comes into awareness. Then there's nobody there. You look at this little "me" that always wants something, or wants to get rid of something. Suddenly it's there in simple awareness. The whole process is suddenly there.

PARTICIPANT 4: I have a question. In all of this it seems like learning is taking place. I'm wondering what this learning process is and what it is that's learning. The most obvious example for me is going back home after retreat and noticing that I'm less reactive, not so driven by habit as before. So it's like I've learned something here, or something has learned something. There's some kind of learning taking place. But it's not intellectual. Is it on a biological level? I don't know. I'm not clear even about my question here.

PARTICIPANT 5: Can the mind come to learn a new way of being, or living?

PARTICIPANT 4: Yes, something like that. I mean my experience is that learning takes place. When you do this kind of work, practice in a sustained way, there's change. So, I'm putting this out to anyone here, and you, Toni. What is learning? Or is anything learning?

TONI: Why make a problem out of it? You say you've noticed that there's learning. Things have changed. I'm not responding as reactively as I did before I came to retreats. So now the brain wants to put it into words, concepts, make it neat. Let it do that, let it say, "I've learned something," or "Something has learned." Can you leave it at that? What more is needed? Just acknowledge that there is learning going on all the time, that it's physical, physiological, mental, a lot of . . . *everything* involved in this. Seeing things differently, seeing the power of image and not falling for it, and so on. This is being learned. Which doesn't mean you won't fall for it again; you may fall again into what has been a strong habit—image formation. Seeing that is also learning—how strong the habits are! How powerful!

PARTICIPANT 6: The temptation for me is to say, "Well, if there is learning going on and it could be made into an equation, a formula, then we could revolutionize the world. Jobs. No more hunger, no more wars." All that. [*pauses*] If I go all the way with it.

TONI: Well, try it! [*much laughter in the group*] Do you have the energy for it?

32

Has Toni Packer Been Totally Transformed?

The moment you begin to see your daily reactions as something to be looked at and wondered about but not instantly identified with—then at that moment you walk lighter.

LET US GO INTO a few questions that are frequently put to me about enlightenment:

"How come I haven't become enlightened after so many years of practice?" "How much longer will it take?" "Is there even such a thing as enlightenment?" "Will I know when it is happening or whether it has already happened?"

Someone wondered if this mysterious attainment has also been called "transformation." She asked, "Is enlightenment the same as the 'total transformation' or 'mutation of the brain cells' that Krishnamurti frequently talked about?"

Let's go into the last question first.

Anyone who has read or heard Krishnamurti knows that he considered "total transformation" ("mutation of the brain cells") the ultimate achievement for human beings. He was certain that a mutation in the brain cells would have to take place for human beings to truly change. It's understandable to wonder what he was referring to with these words.

Several years ago I briefly visited the Krishnamurti Adult Education Center in England, where I had lunch with the man in charge. At one point he said, "I am sorry to say that I have not attained total transformation yet." I don't know how many people who listened to Krishnamurti would say that they have! Mary Luytens, Krishnamurti's biographer, reported in her last volume (*Krishnamurti: The Years of Fulfillment*) that on his deathbed Krishnamurti said, with a touch of sadness in his voice, "Nobody has understood my teaching."

So, last night after the group meeting, I asked myself, "Has there been a total transformation in my life—a palpable 'mutation in the brain cells'? Could I honestly say that to Krishnamurti if he was still alive?"

What came to mind immediately was the fact that I often go to bed with pain, frequently wake up with it, take different medications to alleviate or dull it, and simultaneously feel weighed down with agonizing fatigue. Fortunately none of this has affected the mind in any negative way! When there's a talk to be given or a dialogue to be entered into, speaking in the mode of meditative inquiry, the mind remains sharp, flexible, and creative. This has been one of the miracles of the work of this moment: up until now it has never failed this ailing body. The sickness hasn't gotten any better over the years, but the meditative mind is functioning as well or even better than ever!

So where does "total transformation" and "mutation in the brain cells" fit into this? [*Toni chuckles, then continues seriously again.*] Eyewitness accounts about Krishnamurti's last days state that he frequently screamed with pain. One of his old friends, on his way for a last visit, wrote that he could hear K's pain while approaching the house where he was staying. He was attached to an automatic morphine-drip device that made it possible to bear what is considered to be one of the most excruciatingly painful cancers. One could wonder at this point whether "total transformation of the brain cells" is compatible with screaming from pain.

Maybe there needs to be a change in our ideas about "total transformation" or "mutation in the brain cells," because, as I am presently finding out, the deeper that meditation sinks into silence and motionless wondering, the more sensitive this entire organism grows in many respects. This appears to be one of the transforming aspects of this work: an ever-deepening sensitivity throughout body and mind. Sensitivity not only to the utter beauty of snowflakes sparkling in the sunshine and the fragrance of fresh air wafting through an open window but also to the immense subtleties of pain and physical discomfort—an increasing sensitivity to *everything* inside and out. But that isn't all. I remember now that the person in retreat who asked about "transformation" said that the first Zen book she'd read was Shunryu Suzuki's *Zen Mind, Beginner's Mind*, in which Suzuki distinguishes between "small" self (the mind of samsara) and "big" self (the Unborn, Uncreated Mind).

Actually I go into this phenomenon in an interview with Lenore Friedman in my last book, *The Wonder of Presence*, in a chapter called "Tracking the Two Bodies." This distinction does not arise from superficial thinking. At various times one or the other of two distinct circuits are functioning. For example, let us take the case of taking a leisurely walk through the woods with the mind open and at ease. When an unusually strange sound is heard, it is neither interpreted nor registered as possibly dangerous. At another time, when the mind is closed and restless, the same sound may trigger the cycle of interpretation and fear. Eckhard Tolle speaks about the "pain body." There is indeed a pain body that we know only too well. It's very active, very palpable. I don't know what he calls the "other body," but that's beside the point. The "pain body" senses psychological and physical pain—for instance the pain of jealousy, ambition, or anxiety about the future.

Do you know the poem by Rumi, who centuries ago described a vision of a future desert landscape?

The Tent

Outside, the freezing desert night.
This other night inside grows warm, kindling.
Let the landscape be covered with thorny crust.
We have a soft garden in here.
The continents blasted,
    cities and little towns, everything
    become a scorched, blackened ball.
The news we hear is full of grief for that future,
    but the real news inside here
    is there's no news at all.*

Today this "future" imagined by Rumi has happened in Afghanistan, Iraq, and elsewhere: towns, dwellings, and highways scattered and in shambles. It doesn't have to be imagined. It has happened and reporters' photographs of it are spread throughout our newspapers! So, is the pain body actually nourished through the brain's capacity to imagine anything frightening, threatening, or pleasant?

And yet there is an entirely different way of being when everything appears *completely all right the way it is!* At the instant of total presence (absence of separation), there is no need for the brain to produce phantasmagorias—interpretations of what this could mean to "me," "my" friends, or "my" foes. It is possible to change from interpreting everything according to old patterns of the past, like: "This has always been like this and will always be like this again." That pattern of thinking results in a chokingly narrow world.

There is another possibility of relaxing into not-knowing and not interpreting whatever scenarios have been produced by the

---

* Jalal al-Din Rumi, *The Essential Rumi*, trans. Coleman Barks with John Moyne (New York: HarperCollins, 1995). Used with permission.

conceptualizing brain. It's a giant step! Not from here to there, but right here, on the spot! A giant "step" from the suffering me—suffering from all the actual pains and imagined problems—to *just being* here without knowing, predicting, or reflecting about the past, what it was like or what it meant, or what it means right now. Not that the knowing-mechanism is deleted—it's right here when needed but is not the exclusive function of the brain. When it becomes transparent, it is seen and understood as "just thinking"! Just knowing from memory!

Is that what Krishnamurti meant by a "mutation in the brain cells"? I myself wouldn't use that expression because it doesn't quite feel that way. It is rather experienced as the emergence of a new and different current (or pathway) in the brain. Sensory impulses that enter the brain seem to be conducted in a new and different way. You can directly sense that seeing, hearing, and experiencing arise from the lower abdomen, while the interpretive, cortical region of the brain remains at ease, quietly inactive. Sense impressions aren't automatically conducted to the cortex, which usually raises questions such as "What is this?" "What is it called?" "What does it mean—is it dangerous?" and then searches for appropriate answers. Sounds are just heard, colors and forms simply perceived without immediately having to know their name or what they are or mean. A relaxed mode of not-knowing prevails. Nevertheless, in a truly dangerous situation the need to know the nature of the threat is *not* suppressed, but an intelligent response emerges spontaneously.

Discernment of danger is not asleep! A different conduction of energy takes place. Not necessarily energizing the shoulders and neck, where the "me" functions seem to exert their controlling influence. You can often see how people with a controlling personality, those occupying positions of authority—for instance, generals or defense secretaries—have a stiff upper body, conveying the impression of inflexibility. In the relaxed posture of a meditator, a palpable aliveness can be sensed radiating from below the navel, while the upper body and face express quiet re-laxation and calm.

You might ask a person who is suffering from the pain of a rigid posture (such as an aching, stooped back), "Why don't you bring on that alive body instead of feeling miserably stiff?" It doesn't work quite like that—change doesn't happen just because we want it to! The crucial question is "Am I depressed about my pos-ture, trying to get rid of it through different efforts, or is it intelli-gently understood as what is happening right now due to ten thousand causes and conditions?" Maybe one of the causes for a stooped back is aging! But has one had a glimpse, a fleeting taste, of being without knowing? Being without wanting? Being without fear? Somebody said, "The moment you talk about something de-sirable, such as the feeling of a body without fear—I immediately want it!" Well, you've got it! You don't need to want it! It's just a matter of not going off into thoughts and feelings about the body and its uncertain, dangerous future—the pain body with its phys-ical and psychological hardships!

Yesterday a woman felt overwhelmed by witnessing her own self-loathing, appalled at seeing how greedy she was! But we don't have to become smothered by *what* we see! It's not "me"! It's the human condition, just one of many particular patterns. Each one can reveal itself in a quiet moment. Can we learn, in retreats and in daily life, to see what we see and let it be? Not see it as *my* greed or *my* badness? No! It's not mine. Who would be the owner?

See, everything brings up a new question. Who is the owner of this jealous thought, of this pain body? And don't just say, "I am." Because then I can ask, "What is this 'I'?" Questioning in this man-ner, at first verbally, always thinking, and then . . . the very last question that cannot be answered verbally is just reverberating without knowing! In that way, there is an ever-deepening penetra-tion into the human condition without need for identification. Is it "my" horrible me or "my" wonderful me? It's neither! It's a human being manifesting certain aspects of the whole spectrum of characteristics and sensitivities. The moment you begin to see your daily reactions as something to be looked at and wondered about but not instantly identified with—then at that moment you walk lighter. It's a beautiful word, that word *lighter,* isn't it? It is part of the word *en-light-enment.* Light and light. Not heavy. Not hidden in thick fog.

So, is transformation possible? Has it happened? Ask this when you have been at this for twenty, thirty years. Or immediately, right now. Has Toni changed? Krishnamurti used to confront the people closely around him: "Why haven't you changed?" "Why don't you get this thing?" he would call out (a friend of his told me).

Does describing "the two bodies" help? The conditioned body changes all the time, just as everything conditioned changes every instant. It is conceived, born, grows, matures, propagates, deteriorates, and dies. The Unconditioned is neither conceived nor is it born nor does it die. It is of eternal presence, without qualities such as "good" or "bad," without space such as "huge" or "tiny," and without time such as "past" or "future." The moment the conditioned body lets go of its dominant grip, the Unconditioned manifests as All-encompassing Awareness, Clear Seeing, Absence of Duality, Wholeness, Intelligence, and Compassion.

In the presence of the immense energy of listening and seeing, a conditioned response can be detected before it fully arises in the conditioned body and does its mischief. It can be seen and therefore need not unfold and flower. It can abate in the seeing. The desire to hurt someone verbally or physically in vengeance need not come to fruition—the impulse can abate in the intensity of awareness. However, since the strong presence of seeing is not operating all the time, the conditioned body often works as though on autopilot—blindly, unintelligently, self-centeredly.

That is why it's so very important to come to a place of silence, stillness, and wondering, where one can enter into a quiet, almost motionless not-knowing. In our turbulent daily lives there is hardly any time or space to calm down enough to deeply question and explore the conditioned body—our "bundle of nerves"—to let it show itself for what it is without condemnation or praise. To come to a silent place, together with silent people, everything resonating with vast, boundless presence, waking up to the simple realization that the pain body isn't everything! Awaring here and now is a totally different way of being!

33

Is This All There Is?

We see differently, hear differently, think differently, and keep wanting and fearing when the "me"-circuit is in operation. When the deeply habitual self-referencing—the comparing whatever is perceived in others to "my" performance, "my" idea, "my" accomplishments—begins to slow down and clear the space for simple awareness, a new way of seeing and hearing unfolds. Everything seems to have changed, yet nothing has really changed, except that all of oneself is open, receptive, present, and truly loving. This cannot be practiced—it springs into life as whole and complete being.

How LOVELY IT IS listening to the rain! All of us can partake of this simple wonder together and alone! Is there anything outside of this? It seems that nothing else needs to be said or done while listening to raindrops gently tapping on rooftops and windowpanes.

People hearing me say this frequently ask, "Is this really all there is—just listening to the rain?" Or, after having been repeatedly asked to listen to the songs of birds, retreatants may ask, "Is that what meditation at Springwater is all about—just listening to birds and raindrops? Is it really all, or is there something more?" Friends send me postcards of birds, lovely bird poems, videos displaying their colorful life cycle, and one friend even mailed a small stuffed crow that "caw-caw-caws" happily when pressed on its shiny black breast!

As much as I enjoy these gifts, birds and raindrops are not really the chief focus of Springwater meditative inquiry! [*laughter*] It isn't the content of the listening (such as birdcalls) that matters, but rather its the quality. Likewise in seeing, it is not what is seen that is of importance but the amazing fact that in the wholeness of seeing, the seer may disappear altogether! Do you see what I mean? In complete seeing and hearing the "me" is no longer the driving center, creating a dualistic world. Instead of the experience of "me" and the flower or me and the birdsong, there is just the wholeness of what is heard and seen (touched and tasted)— too marvelous to describe in words: it is the ending of separation!

You've often heard me ask the question "What is this constant wanting and searching for more?" And that's worth going into, isn't it? Can it become increasingly transparent how the "me" is habitually asking for more? Can there be a deepening awareness of "me" constantly wanting more? That's a wonderful practice! Can it come into the full light of awareness? And with deepening awareness, it can actually slow down! The perception of "me" wanting more can actually slow down! It doesn't submit to willpower, as in wanting to have less wanting! It doesn't work that way, as that would just be adding another wanting! What unfolds in awareness is a new, subtle listening that may not ever have been experienced before, because most of the time it has been drowned out by all the other noises taking place in the bodymind. The movement of wanting more often drowns out a subtle, quiet listening, but with increasing awareness one can really hear something, maybe for the first time, because there is no longer this rush of wanting to hear something. Can all the rush of wanting, the silent ambition underneath it, the neediness hiding behind it— can all of that reveal itself in quiet listening and looking? Our motives do reveal themselves when everything slows down in quiet listening.

Watch yourself, and ask occasionally, "Is there a 'me' here?"
Because we can quickly affirm that there's no "me," that we've left
it behind, but we haven't really. It needs sustained awaring, because it sneaks in through the back door: "me" who wants more,
"me" who understands matters, "me" who knows better than the
others, those poor blind people! To keep questioning oneself, not
in order to blame oneself but in order to bring to light all of the
subtle movements of "me" that keep us in the dark. The "me"-
movement is the strongest darkener! We don't see what we're saying and doing because we're darkened, blinded by this "me"-ness.
I'm not talking about literal blindness. A really blind person may
see a lot. This *seeing* is not seeing with the eyes or hearing with the
ears. It perceives with the eyes and ears of the entire universe!

Last night, after supper, I thought I'd do a little bit of writing
since I felt good after a pretty good day. Well, all you have to do is
sit long enough in front of the computer and you don't feel so
good anymore. It started with burning nerve pain throughout the
body that gave rise to the thought "Here you are having a free day
and don't really have to do anything except rest!" I have to keep
telling this to myself because of a deep-seated compulsion to be
doing something all the time—an amazing residue from past conditioning. So I lay down on the sofa, but that didn't help one bit.
I was still "working" on the chapter, and the body was agonizing.
So I went up to the balcony, leaned back in that amazing reclin-
ing chair, and instantly everything discomforting and hurtful disappeared. The pain seemed to be gone and with it every last desire
to feel different. Nothing was left that needed the slightest
change. Just a precious luminous nothing—as portrayed so well
on a birthday card my son had sent me: It shows a broadly smiling
Dalai Lama and a few monks grouped around him. He is holding
a huge parcel in his arms without any bottom to it, and is exclaim-
ing, "It's nothing! That's what I've always wanted for my birthday—NOTHING!"

Right now I can think, talk, and smile about it, but at that moment not a single word came up to disturb this shiny transparent nothing—just a totally radiant hereness-nowness without any thought stirring that "everything is all right." All doubts and explanations had disappeared.

This is what I was trying to get at—and maybe it's too difficult to portray in words—that there is a physical difference in this bodymind when there is openness, hereness, nowness—no-"me"-ness operating. We see differently, hear differently, think differently, and keep wanting and fearing when the "me"-circuit is in operation. When the deeply habitual self-referencing—the comparing whatever is perceived in others to "my" performance, "my" idea, "my" accomplishments—begins to slow down and clear the space for simple awareness, a new way of seeing and hearing unfolds. Everything seems to have changed, yet nothing has really changed, except that all of oneself is open, receptive, present, and truly loving. This cannot be practiced—it springs into life as whole and complete being.

Wisdom, lovingness, and compassion come with abeyance of the ego, the "me." And by this ego-me I don't mean a little ego-entity living inside this body and doing its mischief. Rather, it is our habitually conditioned way of thinking about ourselves, and together with that the emoting. Thinking, "I'm no good," or "I'm not as good as others"—this mobilizes a flood of emotions, stress, and tension, whereas a slowing down of this way of thinking about myself (with no self in operation) calms down emotions, stress, and frustration. Test it! Test it out!

Nothing more needs to happen except—to see clearly! That has its own amazingly gentle and wise action. It can be totally trusted. We have a hard time with it because we're so afraid of standing alone in shame and embarrassment in the face of what we believe others are thinking about us. But others will think what they will regardless of our fears. It preoccupies us constantly to think what others are like or shouldn't be like. This is our Home Box Office! It takes honesty and . . . courage, if you want to use that word . . . to relinquish the defenses. Freedom arises easily with the relinquishing of defenses, because now we can see freely without needing to identify with what is seen. We can see what we are doing without the "Oh, this is the terrible me." We simply observe how human beings respond under conditions of stress and frustration. At one moment it is you reacting, then again me, and at another moment both of us at the same time, from moment-to-moment discovering changing self-images that belong to no one.

Do we need self-images at all? There is such a strong emphasis nowadays on possessing positive self-esteem. And, yes, it is useful to a limited degree—at least it helps if we are constantly putting ourselves down and counteracts the deleterious effects of negative self-images. But why hang on to *any* images, why keep producing them again and again? As someone said the other day, let's not depend on other people to uphold us. It is a precarious addiction, needing other people to tell us how good we are, how loving, and that we are to be appreciated. You can't depend on others to do this for you. (Again, who are the others, and who are you?)

So why not discover that source of goodness and well-being within us? It does not depend on other people telling us what we are. It depends on nothing. It's just in-touch-ness with the source of all living and dying, which is totally trustworthy!

Of course, I can hear some of you say, "I don't have contact with that source. Can you tell me how I can get it, establish it, and keep it?" And the response is, "Always start from not-knowing. Don't start from knowing."

Can we start from the depth of not-knowing—the womb of darkness that is the source of living and dying? It opens eyes and ears. If I do not know, then I am open to what is going on, maybe hearing something never heard before and seeing something never seen before simply because I am here without knowing.

Amazing silence that does not know.

Credits

GRATEFUL ACKNOWLEDGMENT is made to the following for permission to print previously published material:

"Tying Rocks to Clouds" from *Tying Rocks to Clouds: Meetings and Conversations with Wise and Spiritual People*, by William Elliott (Wheaton, Illinois: Quest Books, 1995).

"Firewood Does Not Turn into Ashes" first appeared in *What Is Enlightenment?* magazine, issue 23, Spring/Summer 2003, as part of the article "Enlightenment at the Speed of Life." Reprinted with permission of the publisher.

Response One of "Two Responses to September 11" was originally published in *Inner Directions Journal*. Reprinted by arrangement with Inner Directions, www.innerdirections.org.

Response Two of "Two Responses to September 11" was first published in the Summer 2003 issue of *Buddhadharma*. Reprinted with permission of the publisher.

"The Tent" from *The Essential Rumi*, translated by Coleman Barks with John Moyne, copyright © 1995 by Coleman Barks. Reprinted with permission of the translator.

Books by Toni Packer

The Light of Discovery

To read this book is to enter the essence of our lives and our every-day concerns. Toni Packer shines her gentle light on fear, compassion, impermanence, attraction, prejudice, enlightenment, and much more. As she says, "In truth we are not separate from each other, or from the world, from the whole earth, the sun or moon or billions of stars, not separate from the entire universe. Listening silently in quiet wonderment, without knowing anything, there is just one mysteriously palpitating aliveness." In this work, Packer invites us into our own light of discovery.

The Silent Question: Meditating in the Stillness of Not-Knowing

In *The Silent Question*, Packer provides fresh insights on using the experiences of life that are raw, messy, painful, and sometimes full of laughter to open a way to compassion. She encourages us to let go of our thoughts and to sit "in the stillness of not-knowing" in order to reflect upon the essential question of who we are. Packer encourages us to discover that life, energy, and insight come from the questioning, the looking, the listening.

The Wonder of Presence

In this collection of talks, interviews, and letters, Toni Packer provides a comprehensive overview of the way of meditative inquiry—a nondenominational approach to spiritual work that emphasizes the direct experience of the present moment. "The immense challenge for each one of us," Packer writes, "is can we live our lives, at least for moments at a time, in the wonder of presence that is the creative source of everything?" She shows how we can transform fear, anger, guilt, and attachment to our self-image through simple, direct awareness. Having recently lost her husband of fifty years, Packer also speaks with candor and tenderness about the convulsions of a grieving heart and the peace that undivided awareness can bring.

The Work of This Moment

Toni Packer presents a radically simple and original approach to spiritual growth free from religious authority, doctrine, symbolism, and ceremony. A former Zen teacher and student of Krishnamurti's work, Packer goes beyond traditional religion and explores with the reader the root of human attachments and the source of suffering, opening the way to compassion.